GOAL!

"The Homeless World Cup is a fantastic opportunity and a real inspiration for those taking part. Not only is it an opportunity to improve their health and fitness, but also to be a part of a once-in-a-lifetime experience."

Sir Alex Ferguson

This is sport at its most powerful. True passion, team spirit, grit and glory. The Homeless World Cup is changing lives around the world. Get into the Homeless World Cup and kick off global poverty.

Ian Botham

"The Homeless World Cup is a wonderful event. In the past, it has helped many people change their lives. I fully support this tournament . . ."

Dougray Scott

GOAL!

The Story of the Homeless World Cup

Mel Young

Foreword by Rio Ferdinand

Birlinn

First published in Great Britain in 2005 by
Birlinn Ltd

West Newington House
10 Newington Road
Edinburgh
EH9 1QS

www.birlinn.co.uk

ISBN 10: 1 84158 389 8
ISBN 13: 978 184158 389 1

British Library Cataloguing-in-Publication Data
A catalogue record for this book is available on request from the British Library

Typeset by Hewer Text UK Ltd, Edinburgh
Printed and bound by Thomson Litho, East Kilbride

Foreword

You cannot ignore the power of football. It has the ability to enthral spectators and mesmerise players at the same time. And it can touch all corners of the earth and involve anyone who wants to play, no matter how good or bad they may be.

The Homeless World Cup is inspirational. It has given people who live at the very edge of society an opportunity to prove that they are no different from anyone else. On this new stage they have provided real sporting entertainment and changed the perception of thousands in the process.

They have used football in such a positive way. They have changed themselves – sometimes beyond recognition – but they have enjoyed themselves in the process. And that's what the Homeless World Cup is all about. It's about a unique sporting event which is great fun to watch and be involved in while its real power is in creating positive change.

Football is not only about those players who regularly appear on the television screens. It's about everyone who kicks a ball, no matter if they are in the back streets of Rio or on the grand stages of Nou Camp or the Bernabeu. Football allows you to express yourself and become part of a team at the same time and this happens at any level.

The Homeless World Cup allows people to regain lost self-respect and to wear their colours with pride. It is only the beginning for many people but it makes a crucial difference. The Homeless World Cup will inspire anyone who comes near it and it has the ability to use football to change lives throughout the world.

Rio Ferdinand,
June 2005

Acknowledgements

There are many people I would like to thank. There are too many to mention.

However, I would like to thank all those people who helped me with the research for this book. This involved either setting up interviews with players, having material translated and, in some cases, actually writing some words. They are Monica Sánchez for Spain, Miku Sano for Japan, Luciano Rocco for Brazil, Ron Grunberg for USA, Masha Salivonenko for Poland, James Garner and Pernille Berg for South Africa, Arkady Tuirin for Russia, Paul Gregory for Canada and Bernhard Wolf who helped with the Austrian chapter and compiled the impact report which is covered in the concluding chapter. I must thank my fellow conspirators in the development of the Homeless World Cup: Harald Schmied and Bernhard Wolf. What a team!

Thanks to everyone at INSP, in particular, Lisa Maclean and Shane Halpin for putting up with me and for the rest of the executive – Paula, Nicholas, Jo and Patricia – for allowing me to be sidetracked into all this.

ACKNOWLEDGEMENTS

Thanks particularly to my family, Rona, Graham, Donald and Catriona for giving me such great backing.

Thanks to Polygon/Birlinn for having faith in me. Thanks are particularly due to Neville Moir for his support and Colin McLear for his editorial insight and attention.

There are hundreds of people all over the world who need to be thanked for making the Homeless World Cup actually happen. There are sponsors, organisers, street paper people, individuals who gave their time freely, media people who were so positive, photographers who have granted us free use of their images for our website and this book, government officials who made things happen, politicians, officials with football authorities and at football clubs and you, the supporters. You know who you are. Thank you very much.

The biggest thank you goes to the players. You have every right to stand proud. I love you all.

Viva football. Kick off homelessness.

M.Y.

1

"A hand up, not a hand out"

This book is about a journey. It was to start on the streets of Scotland before extending throughout Europe and across the globe. But it is only a beginning; there is still much distance left to travel.

The first steps were taken in 1993. It was yet another year of Conservative government and there was little in the previous thirteen that offered hope. These were depressing times and I found my conversations increasingly laden with the cries of "where are the solutions?"; "where was the leadership?"; and "why wasn't anybody doing anything?"

We all agreed on how bad things had become. But this was the simple part. There was no one offering answers or seeking to make a positive contribution and it became easy to get lost in the fug of despondency and apathy that had settled upon the country. It was something that we had grown used to and our passive acceptance meant that change was unforeseeable in the near future. We all needed a jumpstart. And mine came in partnership with Tricia Hughes, a friend I had first met some ten years previously.

At that time I was working in a large housing estate on the

outskirts of Edinburgh, having been hired to edit the local newspaper. Tricia was employed as a community development worker and the overall strategy was to create a thriving neighbourhood through empowerment.

At the helm of the project was Laurence Demarco, who oversaw the development programme on behalf of the local council. He was an inspirational figure who was ahead of his time and many of the strategies he was to introduce concerning empowerment and localised control are now part of formal government policy in the UK.

The estate was characterised by high unemployment, a lack of facilities, the growing problem of drug abuse, and underlying poverty that led to feelings of marginalisation and despair. It was typical of many housing schemes in Britain. They were seen as no-go areas and the media was happy to offer examples and enhance their reputations as such. If you were to believe everything you read then these estates were populated by drug-crazed criminals who lived on social security benefits and who would sell your grandmother for the price of a new pair of trainers.

The reality was different, of course. But that doesn't make for good copy. There is a supposed comfort in the stereotyping of people. If they have this background, then they must fit in this box. It is one of the most debilitating parts of life and one most constantly used by the media. Their targets may alter, but the manner of reporting does not and we continue to be willing to characterise and generalise in the most simplistic and obtuse ways. It was this that Tricia and I were to attempt to address come the early 1990s.

I had long since moved on from the community newspaper but throughout the years we had kept in touch and would meet on occasion to catch up on news and gossip, and, inevitably, discuss the way of the world. Negativity was never far from the surface. But there came an evening when we decided to alter the atmosphere of our conversations. Rather than lament the state of the nation, our intention was now to come up with ideas that would lead to the creation of a positive project, no matter how small or ridiculous.

I told Tricia of the time in London when I saw a man selling a newspaper called *The Big Issue*. The vendor was homeless and the idea was that the seller would keep the majority of the cover price, thus alleviating the reliance on charitable handouts. It was not a solution to homelessness by any means, but it was a start. Not least for the vendor as it would begin to address some of the biggest issues inherent in homelessness, those of self-respect, confidence and reintegration.

So, within the context of our plan to "create a positive project", Tricia and I decided to write to Gordon Roddick, the chairman of the Body Shop, who we'd read was behind the *Big Issue* initiative in London. We were to ask about the possibility of starting a similar project in Scotland and his response was to agree to a meeting with his partner, and the real driving force of the venture, John Bird.

The outcome of the first conversation was simple. *The Big Issue* was highly successful in London and growing quickly. As a result they did not have the time or the resources to expand into any other part of the country. Therefore, while John was delighted that we wanted to start in Scotland, it was clear that this would happen only if we were to set up our own company, raise the finance ourselves and create a separate magazine. There would be links to the London operation but, in effect, we would be independent. It was the creation of the first-ever social franchise.

Within three months of this meeting, Tricia and I had written the business plan, left our jobs and raised the initial capital to fund the magazine. In addition to harrying family and friends, we had introduced a scheme of founding sub-scribers whereby people bought an expensive subscription to the magazine even though a first edition had yet to be printed. Their belief only instilled further confidence within us that we were doing the right thing.

The Big Issue in Scotland was launched in June 1993, as a fortnightly magazine. It sold for 50p with the vendor retaining 60% of the cover price. The principle was simple. The potential seller would come into the office, and once it was established they were homeless, each would be given a starter pack of ten magazines to sell. Once all were sold, they would be able to purchase further copies for 20p. It was a traditional wholesale/retail operation and one that continues to this day. The magazine has grown and is now published weekly and retails at £1 but the vendor continues to retain 60% of each sale.

The philosophy of the magazine was embedded from first publication and was based around the slogan "A Hand Up, Not A Hand Out". We wanted to illustrate that the homeless were not simply a statistic, but were individuals, and we wished to present them not as numbers but as people. There was a need to create an alternative to begging, and it was essential to alter the landscape in terms of attitude and interaction.

Homelessness strips away self-respect and destroys confidence. A person feels disconnected, becomes outcast from normality and self-worth inevitably crumbles. *The Big Issue in Scotland* hoped to address this through the simple process of selling a street magazine. It offered the opportunity of reintegration by giving the vendor control of their destiny, and supplying a routine to their day.

A vital part of this process is the transaction, when the homeless and the 'have' world connect. It is the briefest of moments when society acknowledges the presence of the vendor and their attendant problems. They are no longer invisible and a tiny bridge is built where both the buyer and seller can see the other side. As soon as that happens, a new dimension to life and its possibilities emerges. The more connections that are made, the more likely real change will take place. And the magazine was to make an immediate impact.

The first edition of *The Big Issue in Scotland* sold out its printing of 25,000 copies. For the next twelve months, we kept increasing the print run to match demand. At one point we sold 140,000 copies of one edition. And it continued selling out. In part, this was due to the magazine being so readable, something we had striven for. It combined social comment through stories and features with news about arts and entertainment. As it grew we were able to carry out investigative stories and campaigns which won the magazine media awards and early recognition from within the industry. We had no intention of it becoming a "pity purchase".

But I also believe that the essence of its success was just being in the right place at the right time. If we were to launch in 2005, the idea might have worked but I doubt whether it would have been as successful. Back then, buying the magazine became a badge of protest, especially amongst the young, and was indicative of the general public's distaste for the prevailing political atmosphere. People wanted change. They were shocked by the growing number of homeless on the streets of Scotland and they saw no opposition, no alternative and no interest coming from the Government.

In addition, we had a ready-made workforce, eager to work for the money that would help remove them from their predicament. And we also appealed to all political creeds: the Left, because we were apparently defying the Government and highlighting their ignorance of the problems; and the

Right because we were following market principles and were not seeking hand-outs from the Government. These factors lifted the magazine to dizzy sales heights which we could only have dreamed about.

The atmosphere has since changed. Scotland has its own Parliament and has a governing body that is committed to an agenda which includes dealing with social issues such as homelessness. Indeed, they have passed legislation and put resources behind an ambitious plan to end the problem altogether by 2008.

The Big Issue in Scotland, however, continues to be successful. 30,000 copies a week are sold and we run a number of associated projects. It has become part of the urban landscape of Scotland and is respected throughout the world for what it has achieved and continues to achieve.

The mid-nineties saw a huge growth in *Big Issue* magazines across the UK. Separate editions began to appear in Wales, the North and in the South-West of England and combined sales reached over 400,000 a week. It was a simple concept and it proved to be very effective. It was no surprise, therefore, that its success was noted beyond Britain. Enquiries came from people interested in mirroring the *Big Issue* concept in other countries.

The journey had really begun.

2

"We do it when the electricity works"

It was March 1996 and I was in St Petersburg, Russia. There was little I had been told that could have fully prepared me for what I was to see. The collapse of the Soviet system, its move towards the extremities of harsh market economics and the lack of a welfare system, meant that many were forgotten, ignored and abandoned. People were left to fend for themselves and unofficial figures suggested that 3,000 homeless people were dying each year. I was horrified by what was unfolding. But there was also cause for hope. It came in the form of a project called Nochlezhka, which I had come to know of through my work with the International Network of Street Papers (INSP).

The INSP was formally launched in 1995. It sought to represent the interests of its members to the outside world, as well as helping to support and develop the various street publications that had begun to sprout up across Europe. Sixteen newspapers were to put their signatures to the Street Paper Charter. By 2005, membership had grown to forty-two, representing every continent in the world. The papers have a combined annual sale of nearly 25 million and thousands of homeless and long-term unemployed people use the papers to earn a living and help break the cycle of poverty.

The Big Issue in Scotland had been one of the founding organizations of the INSP. With its headquarters situated in Glasgow, there was an opportunity for me to become increasingly active in the international development of the street paper movement. There was obvious excitement. While I naturally supported aid where necessary, I was against the culture of dependency it created in the long term. It smacked of patronage and control, with overtones of the worst aspects of colonization, whereby Western nations presume to know what is best. Real solutions are based upon self-determination, genuine partnerships and the philosophy of "a hand up, not a hand out". In the INSP movement I could see the potential for creating a major change in thinking towards tackling poverty on a global scale. It was in Russia that I became convinced.

At the inaugural INSP conference in 1995, the situation regarding homeless people in St Petersburg was harrowingly related. On the basis of these stories, a fundraising campaign in Scotland was organized. It would raise £10,000, which would be used to establish a street paper in the Russian city. In the company of Bill Gilmour, a Glasgow *Big Issue* vendor who had played a significant role in the campaign, I travelled to St Petersburg.

On our first morning, we walked to the Nochlezhka (English translation 'Night Shelter') office and we witnessed our hosts picking up twigs and pieces of wood along the way. They were not to be used for warmth. Although set on fire, they were positioned under frozen street pipes in order to melt the ice. This was then mixed with the concentrated soup that had been handed out earlier.

At the Nochlezhka centre, there was already a long, ragged

line of homeless people. The project worked in spartan conditions with no running water and an electrical system that came and went often. I wondered aloud as to how they could produce a newspaper in such conditions.

"Easy," was the response. "We do it when the electricity works."

Bill and I watched as the queue for soup grew. And then he disappeared. A few minutes later, Bill returned clutching as much bread as he was able to carry. He had walked into a baker's store and spent all of his money. It was to provide a sight I will never forget – the smile on his face and the look of delight on everyone else's. Bill's act of kindness has gone down in the city's folklore and was the beginning of a real connection between a street newspaper from Scotland and one in Russia.

Their overall strategy was simple. Nochlezhka had seen how the street papers had worked in the UK and wanted to create something similar in St Petersburg. They set up the soup kitchen, which offered basic nourishment, and then would try to persuade the homeless people to move onto selling the newspaper which was called *The Depths* – it would change its name to *Put Domoi* ('*Journey Home*') in 2003. It seemed to be working. Selling just five copies would provide enough for food and possibly a bed somewhere. But it was also all about changing attitudes as well. The content was similar to other street papers, mixing serious articles along with coverage of the arts scene. It was alternative without being subversive.

The homeless people in Russia were different from the Scots. Many were much older, some even at an age when they should be drawing a pension. And too many seemed resigned to their situation. Nochlezhka was intent on altering this outlook. In the meantime, I sat and listened to the stories of the street.

Igor is a large man, a caricature of a Russian. He has a huge, scraggly beard and a traditional bearskin hat that sits atop a greasy mop of long, unkempt hair. There are many others like him. He is surrounded by those who have not washed for weeks and whose lives are soundtracked by hacking coughs. Tuberculosis is rife amongst the homeless people in Russia and it is clear that my interpreter is uncomfortable.

Igor explains that he had been at university, where he excelled at physics. He had, however, fallen foul of the Soviet regime and was transported to a gulag in some far-flung outpost of the Russian empire. Igor doesn't know how many years he was there. Decades, perhaps. His release was sudden and he was sent back to St Petersburg, the city of his birth, with no money and no papers. Without the appropriate documentation, Igor had little prospect of work or housing. He survives by coming to the soup kitchen.

There was little bitterness or anger about Igor. While I would have seethed with the injustice of it all, he simply wanted to talk about philosophy, fate and destiny. He confirmed that life was full of twists and turns, and explained that in such circumstances you should always seek to learn. There was no room for resentment.

The system of an internal passport, or *propiska*, is a constant cause of homelessness and exclusion within Russia. Without the *propiska*, you have no entitlements. You cannot work and have no right to shelter or any welfare payment. According to the State, you do not exist. In Igor's case, he was simply not given papers upon his release. He'd been away for so long that he couldn't prove to the authorities who he was. Igor's case, unfortunately, was not unusual.

I also listened to the story of a man who had been drafted into the Russian army. This was at the time of the first war in Afghanistan. When his unit was disbanded, he was sent back to St Petersburg and informed that his papers would be sent on. Months passed and without the paperwork, effectively a non-person in the eyes of the authorities, he became homeless. There was little prospect of his documentation ever arriving and so it proved.

Nochlezhka, though, were to organise their own system. A desk was set up in their offices where homeless people could register and be given a paper similar to the *propiska*. This was sanctioned by the government of St. Petersburg in 1999 and they were to set up its own registering points in 2000.

St Petersburg had proved a special experience. A real bond had been created between our "two families" and Bill and I returned to Scotland with a determination to not only build upon this specific partnership, but attempt to do likewise elsewhere. With the support of the British Government and other organisations, similar projects begin to form across Eastern Europe. *The Big Issue in Scotland* developed links with the production of street newspapers in the Ukraine, Romania, the Czech Republic, Poland, Slovakia and Hungary.

The INSP has grown quickly since its formation. With each and every new member, its impact can be seen where it most matters – on the street. Its purpose is to help and a vital part of the organisation is its annual conference when representatives from each paper come together for moral support, exchange of ideas and the formulation of new thinking. These gatherings would bring an extra dimension to our work and we would return to our respective papers fuelled with energy and in-spiration. But we were all editors, and board members. What about our vendors? If only there was a way they could experience something like this . . .

3

"What's football got to do with it, just build more houses"

Like many of the best ideas, it came during a conversation in a bar. In this instance, the setting was a beach establishment in Cape Town, following the close of the sixth annual INSP conference in 2001. I was seated with Harald Schmied, a representative of the Graz street newspaper *Megaphon*, and Peter Ten Caat from *Straat*, which was published in Utrecht. As would often happen, issues pertinent to the conference would spill over into more informal surroundings. The issue under discussion was that of international partnerships and exchange.

It was agreed that the conferences fostered a "can do" atmosphere that carried the delegates through the year to come. Possibilities would become realities and we wondered how our vendors, the homeless sellers, could become part of this. If they could see, hear and participate in such an experience on a yearly basis, then they would feel the invigoration we felt. And this could be translated onto the streets.

We talked of organising vendor exchanges between countries. It was possible. However, there were a number of obstacles. How could we get a Russian vendor across Europe if he or she wasn't even recognized by their own authorities? Visa restrictions, employment laws and social security issues would cause additional headaches. And there was also the problem of communication. It was then that football was mentioned.

The game was an international language, someone said. People understood the simplicity of football and could play the game easily without needing to understand a word of the opposition side. This was the answer, we quickly concluded: organise matches between teams representing street newspapers.

"Very well," I said. "Some of our vendors play together. We'll take on anyone who wants to play."

"We have a team attached to *Megaphon*: play us," replied Harald and as the night rolled on, the idea grew. *Megaphon* would now represent Austria, and we would play on behalf of Scotland. Other teams would have to become involved, indeed, many teams, all competing for a single trophy and representing their respective nations. The dream of the Homeless World Cup was born but the real challenge lay in turning it into some kind of reality. In the process, we would have to convince our colleagues, who demonstrated scepticism when first told.

I left Cape Town intoxicated by the general success of the conference and my imaginings of the football tournament. Harald felt likewise. He was dedicated to his work at *Megaphon*, which he had joined in October 1998. The paper is backed by Caritas, the biggest social organization in Austria and run by the Catholic Church. In Graz alone, it has over 800 employees and 70 projects. These include children's care, refugees for women, homeless shelters and drug and alcohol therapy centres. Caritas is an integral part of life in Austria, as it is in many other European countries.

Apart from his commitment to social issues, sport runs

through Harald's blood. Football is his first love and he had played semi-professionally for a number of years. He gave this up upon the birth of his first son, but he continued with other activities such as skiing and canoeing. This involvement in sport convinced Harald of its potential in involving lots of people, no matter their background, and creating a positive outcome. It was simply a question of providing the right parameters. I was easily convinced.

In the months following the 2001 conference, Harald and I began to imagine how the event would come together. We spoke to a range of people, seeking advice and looking for feedback. Though the response was generally positive, many didn't view it as practical. Others couldn't see what the benefits would be and once more I was to hear the question I had regularly been asked since I began working with homeless people:

"Just build more houses; end of problem, isn't it?"

If only it was so clear-cut. While organising a house provides an answer to a situation, it doesn't necessarily supply the whole solution. Homelessness in the West is characterised by a lack of accommodation and money but it is also married to alienation and marginalisation. The more people have been ground down by the system and the longer they have been abandoned, the more it takes to reintegrate them into society.

In the UK, for example, a significant proportion of those people becoming homeless have been previously been brought up "in care", a British term for living in a children's home. The Government is now fully aware of this issue and works closely with those leaving care. However, if someone falls through the net, it is easy to become homeless at a very young age. Simply giving someone a house at this stage is not a solution because they are potentially so disorientated that they have no idea how to survive.

I remember well the experiences of a man who was aged only seventeen when he first started selling *The Big Issue in Scotland*. He had obvious intelligence, allied to a sharp wit and a willingness to help. Yet he found it difficult to read and write and perceived himself to be an outcast. We would find him a house but he only ever lasted a couple of days, always citing some excuse to explain why he was back sleeping on the streets.

It was in the early days of the magazine and we couldn't work out exactly what the problem was. At the same time, we were beginning to test the patience of the housing agencies we were working with.

The issue was simple, however. He found it much safer to be on the streets. That is where he was most at ease. For those of us who live in the housed world, the streets represent a dangerous and terrifying place. Reality shows that this can be true, but for this young man, the thought of living in a house was just as troubling. But he always said that's where he wanted to be. The challenge, therefore, was to work with him to create a path from the street to a house. It wasn't easy and was often characterised by lows when he suddenly "self-destructed" and fled.

There was a time when he had settled into what seemed to be the perfect flat for him. It was central and he shared with other people – something he was keen on. They were all students and it suited everyone perfectly. One of the bedrooms, however, had always been empty as a student had been at school abroad for a while. On the eve of this individual's return, the young man disappeared back onto the streets.

When asked about what had happened, he told me that he had been apprehensive about the student's return. Though never having met them, he had convinced himself that the returning student wouldn't like him, meaning that he had to get out immediately, despite loving his flat and the people who stayed there.

"This is ridiculous," I said, "Everyone likes you."

But it was too late. I wanted to weep and scream in frustration. And so it goes on. Thousands of homeless people who are marginalised by society find it so difficult to re-integrate. The process can take a long time and cannot be solved by simply throwing people into houses. I try to explain this to people who suggest solutions are found in building houses. I tell them of the individual stories. And I urge that they speak to homeless people and listen with an open ear.

The street paper provides a platform where homeless people can earn a living. For some, it is not enough. Other projects are required. And playing football was to become one of them. Harald and I were determined to achieve that.

4

"You're crazy anyway, do the opposite of what appears to be totally sensible . . . it's what you people do"

No one ever said it was going to be easy. There were over 500 other projects jostling for recognition and the organising committee had thus far been unimpressed with the presentation. They demonstrated little understanding of what was being suggested, and were unable to see the benefits it would bring to the city. The project was close to being lost and Harald needed to act quickly.

From his bag, he began to produce a copy of every street newspaper from around the world.

"The people of Brazil will see Graz."

"The people of England will see Graz."

"The people of Russia will see Graz."

"The people of Hungary will see Graz."

"The people of Sweden will see Graz."

By the time Harald had shown thirty street newspapers, the scepticism that had previously filled the room had dissipated. The committee had been impressed by the global reach of the INSP and the Homeless World Cup had found its host.

Graz had been named the 2003 European Capital of Culture. Since this announcement, Harald and his colleagues had begun discussing ways in which homeless people could become involved. It was a platform to prove that people, regardless of their background and circumstance, could play a role in such an event. Further thought brought Harald to the conclusion that this would the perfect opportunity for the inaugural Homeless World Cup.

As one of the official, recognised projects of the Capital of Culture, it meant that certain key parts of the city's infrastructure would become available: marketing, the press centre, linkage to government agencies behind the programme and the provision of a little money.

It was little wonder that Harald arrived at the 2002 INSP conference in Madrid brimming with confidence. He provided an animated talk to our delegates and offered the World Cup as a symbol of grass-roots globalisation whereby you could improve your life situation by playing a game. Enthusiastic discussions were to follow about rules, travel arrangements, funding and eligibility. The tournament was no longer a dream and the road to Graz had begun. Or so we thought. The news that came in January 2003 brought us face to face with a harsh reality.

Harald and his Austrian colleagues had applied for a grant of €160,000 from the European Union to cover the costs of the event. The lengthy application form had been submitted on time and officials at the EU had been encouraging. They said our project fitted the criteria for such grants and the overall integration objectives of the organisation. It was intimated that we could expect a positive outcome and sure enough, our application proved successful. In one frantic phone call, however, this was subsequently retracted. Apparently the British Government had objected to a technical point on which the funding scheme was based. Officials at the EU were clearly embarrassed, while the Austrian authorities were furious. We were simply stunned. There was now a huge hole in our funding requirements and we had less than six months to make it up if we were to proceed. Worse was to follow.

With the event only months away, the phone rang. It was Harald. He spoke in his usual jovial manner.

"You aren't going to believe this but I'm phoning from the intensive care ward – I've had a major heart attack."

My reaction was one of disbelief. Harald was a young man in his early thirties and an active sportsman. It took him several minutes to persuade me that he was telling the truth. Harald had collapsed while playing football. But true to form, he wasn't calling to tell me simply about himself. He informed me that everything regarding the Homeless World Cup was in order and that he had already found a replacement.

I was stunned. Doubts began to enter my mind. My main partner, who was the crucial local organiser, was lying in a hospital bed; we were still way short of our funding target; and, just to increase the woe, my two fellow INSP board members had had to step aside. One contracted hepatitis after eating shellfish and required time for recuperation, while the other decided to resign due to other work commitments. I felt as if I was the last man standing!

All logic told me that the event should be cancelled. I had a conversation with myself in the mirror. The mirror told me to stop. I spoke at length with Layla Mathers, who acted as the INSP secretary and was my colleague in the international department of *The Big Issue in Scotland*.

"All logic says we should stop but there is something about all of this which I feel is significant and therefore I've concluded that we should just proceed, which is totally crazy, I know, but there's something telling me this is going to work out. What do you think?"

I awaited her response. If she had been at all negative, I think I would have called Harald to recommend that we cancel.

"You're crazy anyway," Layla replied. "Do the opposite of what appears to be totally sensible and make things happen. It's what you people do."

And it's what we did. No longer did I harbour any thoughts of postponement. It seemed as though others thought likewise. The Graz authorities were so taken aback by the European Union decision that they decided to pull out all the stops to make the event happen and acquire the necessary funding. Despite some initial wariness, they had seen the potential of the Homeless World Cup and were able to gather the funds that we had been missing. Around two-thirds of the money came from varying government departments, with the rest hailing from private sector sponsorship.

It had previously been agreed that Harald and his team would be responsible for all matters Austrian. With Harald in hospital, Bernhard Wolf took over the reins at the Austrian end. This meant taking care of the financial aspect, the hosting of the tournament and looking after the players from the moment they arrived in Graz to the time they left. My work was on the international side. Among other things, I needed to ensure the players were able to travel without hindrance.

While progress had initially been marked by disappointments, both financial and health-related, there were other matters that had provided encouragement. In January 2003, I was taking part in the annual meeting of the World Economic Forum in the village of Davos, Switzerland. I had been invited to participate because of my connection with the Schwab Foundation for Social Entrepreneurship. In 2001 I had been recognised by the Foundation for my work as a social entrepreneur around the world and this selection meant, among other things, that I could participate in the WEF's annual meeting.

During the series of plenary sessions and workshops that characterise the Forum, I was persuaded by Adolf Ogi, the former President of Switzerland, and one of the Schwab Foundation Board members, to go along to an evening discussion on sport. Mr Ogi is now the United Nations special advisor to Kofi Annan on Sports and Peace, believing passionately in the power of sport in overcoming many of the world's problems.

At the session we were seated around tables and were invited to listen to the opening speeches. At the end of the evening, we were encouraged to respond, therefore over dinner we became involved in intense discussions, everyone detailing their interest in sport and its potential on a broader scale. I contributed by explaining the story of the Homeless World Cup.

When the time came for each table to articulate their thoughts to the room, Vivienne Redding, the Commissioner for Sports at the European Union, stood up. She was to talk on our behalf. Unknown to me at this time was the fact that she had been the person in charge when we had made our unsuccessful grant bid to the EU.

"Well, I had prepared some words," she started. "But this gentleman on my left has a much better story to tell."

Vivienne was referring to me. All of a sudden I had the ears of the room. With no prepared speech, I offered an abridged version of the hopes behind the Homeless World Cup, which was received with thunderous applause. Vivienne was to explain later that she had known of our proposal and had thought it to be a fine idea. She apologised about being unable to provide funding while assuring me that it had been taken out of her hands. The very least she could do was to give me the floor for a couple of minutes. It was a gesture that was certainly appreciated and one that would reap dividends.

Sitting at one of the other tables was Phil Knight, the

chairman and co-founder of Nike. Following my brief presentation, we spoke and he suggested I contact their Corporate Social Responsibility department in Brussels. In April they confirmed that Nike would be making a contribution of €50,000 towards the Homeless World Cup. Naturally, this was a cause for celebration. It meant that teams from Africa and South America, who were struggling to make the event, could now participate. Combined with the confirmation of the Austrian funding, the tournament was financially secure. Flights were being booked, train tickets bought, and minibuses prepared. All roads were leading to Graz. The first Homeless World Cup was to kick-off on July 7th, 2003. And something very special was about to take place.

5

*"Compulsive viewing, good fun and [it] makes
a genuine impact on one of today's most
intractable social problems"*

For an event like the Homeless World Cup to make a real
impact it had to be taken seriously. We needed endorsement
from the corporate world and from the football authorities.

The support from Nike was crucial for the event. Not only
did it give us the finance we needed but with their reputation as
one of the world's leading sports brands, it gave the whole
event credibility.

The same applied to UEFA, football's governing body in
Europe. Harald had approached them earlier in the year after
he had discovered they had a special fund which gave grants to
community initiatives.

What was so impressive was how both UEFA and Nike were
prepared to back the event before the first tournament had taken
place. We had been very confident in our approach but companies and institutions tend to hang back rather than supporting
new initiatives. What both UEFA, from the football side, and
Nike, from the corporate side, were doing was backing innova-
tion in sport and for this they should be heartily applauded.

Lars-Christer Olsson, UEFA's chief executive, said that "the award was made because we are committed to supporting football initiatives in the community and also because we think this tournament will genuinely help tackle exclusion."

The proposal fitted in well with UEFA's overall aims for promoting the game to all sections of the community. In recent years, football has become perceived as a rich man's game, and has been criticised for losing touch with its grass roots. Too often, its image is that of the lavish lifestyle enjoyed by the very few professionals who make millions out of the game. These stars have become celebrities and tabloid fodder. The stadiums are full of corporate boxes and entrance fees grow ever higher. There's a real danger that football might detach itself from the very people who love the game: the fans.

Football used to be played in the street by youngsters. It's where they learned their basic skills. In many cities, that's just not permissible or possible. Schools are not so keen to promote the game, while playing fields are being sold for property development.

Burn away the grass roots and you'll eventually have nothing to feed into the game. UEFA not only have a role to promote and govern the professional game but they have a vital responsibility to maintain football at all levels. They are very active in supporting community initiatives, particularly amongst young people, because this can benefit the community in all manner of positive ways – kids stay of out potential trouble and the health benefits are obvious.

UEFA are genuinely keen to promote football as a game for everyone. Thus, they promote a number of different projects, and have four core organisations with four themes:

- FARE, Football Against Racism in Europe, targets racism in all forms

- CCPA, Cross Cultures Project Association, is aimed at children, grass-roots football and promotes peace in the Balkans and the Caucasus
- SOEE, Special Olympics Europe Eurasia and their Football Development Programme supports disabled football
- ICRC, International Committee of the Red Cross is involved with children who have been the victims of war, through their Protect Children at War campaign.

It is a well thought-out strategy which supports those who are marginalised. Much of the finance for these initiatives comes from the fines imposed by UEFA on clubs and players who break the rules. These days when I hear that a club or a player is in trouble with UEFA, I wish for a fine rather than a ban. I know the money is going the right way. The richer the club the better it feels.

In addition, UEFA runs an assistance programme which is available to all its 52 member associations. Called HatTrick, it helps finance the infrastructure of development projects, including education and the construction of mini-pitches in each country.

From the corporate perspective, Nike has similar objectives.

"Nike has in place community programmes worldwide, in keeping with its pledge to plough back approximately 3% of pre-tax profits in to the community," said a company spokesman.

"This money is not to be used for marketing, such as promoting sporting events, so when Nike was first approached about sponsoring the 2003 Homeless World Cup it was initially viewed with scepticism. But after looking carefully at the event and its goals, Nike decided it was a programme it should support."

"The event was only the tip of the iceberg," explained Hannah Jones, Director of Corporate Responsibility for Nike

EMEA. "We came to realise that this could have long-term impact. It's a way of mobilising and bringing people into an environment of teamwork and commitment."

After the event Nike admitted that agreeing to sponsor the tournament had been a big risk for them.

"These guys had never done this before and this had the potential to be the biggest disaster ever. So we thought: 'We like that! We like people with crazy ideas'. Because we are a young company and not very bureaucratic, we are often able to fund people and projects that couldn't get funded elsewhere."

Other companies came on board with their kind support. White and Case with law offices all over the world were able to give us much-needed legal advice. DHL helped disseminate tournament information to the teams and the media throughout the world and Salesforce.com gave us access to software which helped with database management and planning.

All these companies have clear policies of Corporate Social Responsibilities and take their role in society very seriously. They realise that the planet cannot survive unless everyone is putting something back – businesses included.

Critical journalists sometimes ask if the support we receive is not just a cynical public relations ploy on behalf of big business and the sporting authorities to make them look good and to detract from genuine criticism about their size and profitability.

Every sporting event is supported by sponsors and advertising and the Homeless World Cup is no different. Just like the others, without sponsorship the Homeless World Cup would not exist. Neither would the World Cup for that matter. Journalists don't ask the same question to the organisers behind the Champions League, so why do they ask us?

"The Homeless World Cup is dealing with people who are totally marginalised in society and it could be argued that the very people who are supporting you, are the ones who have caused these problems in the first place," is a fairly standard riposte.

There is a tenuous link but it is more a question of the role of all businesses in society. We were building something which was very practical and that could make a difference to the lives of the people participating. We weren't creating something to change the economic system in the world. The Homeless World Cup wasn't a revolution but we hoped it would bring about lasting change. And you can't do that in isolation.

Since the first Homeless World Cup all of our sponsors have stayed with us. They were very pleased with the outcome, its impact and the profile it created which, in turn, highlighted their community initiatives.

"The success of the Homeless World Cup is built on the enormous power of football in social inclusion," announced Lars-Christer Olsson, UEFA's chief executive in a statement.

"The world's most famous team sport can definitely help people to move on in life. The Homeless World Cup has set up a new frame for the empowerment of homeless people. The dynamics of the event have been driven by the international media, who have made the Homeless World Cup a well recognised event.

"Consequently, the Homeless World Cup aims to bring up a new image of homeless people in the world. The UEFA is very keen to be a patron of this excellent initiative."

Ringing endorsements like this from one of the world's most powerful bodies gave us great confidence and helped to open doors. We had gained credibility and our profile had risen quite dramatically.

"The impact of the Homeless World Cup has been tremendous and we would like to work with the people behind it over the next three years to make it become sustainable," explained the new Director of Corporate Responsibility for Nike EMEA, Maria Bobenrieth.

"We are particularly interested in the effect this has on the ground in each country and we face an exciting challenge to replicate the impact across the globe."

"We are genuinely delighted to be involved with a tournament which is compulsive viewing, good fun and makes a genuine impact on one of today's most intractable social problems."

6

"[He] looked like a rap artist or film star,
rather than a goalkeeper in a street soccer
competition"

By July 6th, all of the eighteen teams had arrived in Graz:
Germany, Holland, South Africa, Wales, Spain, Sweden, USA,
Slovakia, Switzerland, Russia, Ireland, Denmark, England,
Poland, Italy, Brazil, Scotland and, of course, Austria. For
many of the participants, it was the first time they had been out
of their respective cities, let alone in a foreign land.

A school had been transformed into the 'players' village' for
the week and each squad had been allocated a classroom as a
dormitory. Meals were provided in the canteen and medical
facilities were also on hand. And as the school was set in
substantial grounds, there was plenty of space for the teams to
train, relax and mingle with each other.

The opening ceremony was to prove a moving occasion.
The placid Sunday afternoon usually known to Graz was
punctured by a cacophony of joyous noise as the teams,
waving a multitude of flags, made their way through the
city's streets. Applause from waiting spectators and dig-

nitaries greeted their arrival in the town's main square and one by one each team stepped forward upon the playing of their national anthem. The USA decided that Jimi Hendrix provided the most appropriate rendition of 'The Star Spangled Banner'.

The teams wore their national colours and had the blessing of their respective football associations. And while some wore exact replicas, others took the strips and added their own sponsor's logo or simply advertised the name of their street newspaper. Every player wore their uniform with pride. Badges were kissed and each identified with the country they represented, perhaps surprisingly. Surely they had a right to be angry with their circumstances at home and the authorities' failure to address the issues. But no. This was all about playing for your country.

With anticipation, the draw was then made. There were to be four qualifying groups, two of four teams and two of five, each side playing the others in their section twice. Unlike other major football competitions, however, we had no way of knowing who the good teams and who the minnows were. Just because a squad came from a nation which had a professional reputation, this did not necessarily mean that it would translate into the performance of the homeless team. Thus, every side was thrown into the hat.

Holland and Germany were drawn together, causing "oohs" and "aahs" to emanate from the crowd, who were acutely aware of the rivalry that exists between the two nations. The Scots laughed ironically when placed in the same section as Brazil, something which seems to happen with regularity at the professional World Cup. But while the latter always triumphed on those occasions, who knew what was to happen this time around.

With the football scheduled to begin the following day, the squads returned to the village to rest, prepare and keep an eye on the opposition's training sessions. Following a conversation in a bar in South Africa, we had now reached the stage when it was less than twenty-four hours before the first ball of the inaugural Homeless World Cup would be kicked. Action was now to speak louder than all our words.

Street soccer is a game that places the emphasis on skill and speed. And these are its basic rules:

The playing area measures 20 by 10 metres and the surrounds are made of wooden hoardings, which can be utilised when passing the ball. The surface is that of any street – concrete, though there is a special felt area laid only for use by the goalkeeper. In addition, there are three outfield players and a further four substitutes that can be revolved as many times as necessary. The game consists of 7-minute halves, supervised by a qualified referee who sits on a chair overlooking the court, rather like a tennis umpire. When players are shown a blue card for foul play, they remain in the sin-bin for two minutes. A red card, as in the 11-a-side game, results in expulsion for the rest of the match.

In Graz, the main court had been erected in the main square, and could accommodate nearly 1,200 spectators. A second, smaller arena was placed nearby and games would take place simultaneously. The matches would start in the early afternoon and continue into the evening, and due to the non-stop manner of play, it provided an extremely exciting form of entertainment for all who watched.

One of the first matches on court was the clash between Holland and Germany. No-one knew the standard of the two teams but given their history, much was expected. The crowd was ready for a close and tense encounter but it was not to materialise, with the Dutch romping home 14:0. The following evening would provide a similar one-sided affair, with the Germans suffering a 12:1 defeat.

Traditionally, games between these two nations have been marked by ugliness and aggression. In Graz, however, this was not to be the case. At the end of their second match, the Dutch goalkeeper was to rush towards his German counterpoint and hoist him upon his shoulders. To great applause and much appreciative foot-stamping from the spectators, they made a lap of the arena. This gesture and resultant crowd reaction was one of the first tangible signs that something distinctive was unfolding.

Holland were to continue unbeaten through Group A, with additional successes over South Africa and Wales. The Germans would ultimately find themselves at the foot of the table while the South Africans would comfortably overcome Wales to secure second place.

Group B was made up of teams whose players, by their own admission, were not necessarily the best at soccer. Whatever they might have lacked in skill, however, they certainly made up for in entertainment. And the crowds were quickly to fall in love with Sweden, Switzerland, Spain, Slovakia and USA.

The Swiss were to lose all of their games, concede 65 goals and manage to score only five – each greeted with a roar that was big enough to grace any major stadium in Europe. Many of the squad were recovering from drug and alcohol problems but had spent a great deal of time training in the lead-up to the tournament. They were obviously trying their best and loving every moment of their participation. And the crowd smiled each time they heard the sound of cow bells and the Swiss team strode onto the court. But they were never laughing at the side that appeared before them. Rather, they were laughing with them and a real bond was being created between the Swiss and the spectators. People seemed to know instinctively where the players were coming from and appeared to identify closely with their struggles. Barriers were being torn down. And applause sounded out for the participants' efforts. The losses on the field were of no consequence.

The USA were also to prove as popular. The squad hailed from New York and had been uncertain about what they were undertaking even as their training progressed and the tournament began. They harboured fears that they would lose every game to their more football-wise counterparts and the crowd warmed to their naivety and honesty.

Team USA were determined to perform as well as they could. And they reached out to the spectators, particularly the goalkeeper, Rory Levine, who would end every match by rushing to the crowd and high-fiveing everyone. Dressed in trendy sunglasses with a bandana wrapped around his skull, Levine looked like a rap artist or film star, rather than a goalkeeper in a street soccer competition, especially one that was for homeless people. And the youngsters loved him for it.

Another character was Harris Pankin. Looking like a throwback to the days of Woodstock, Harris had a mass of unruly hair, scraggly beard and John Lennon-style rounded glasses which he insisted on wearing during the matches. He rushed around the arena demanding penalties, incurring the wrath of referees and immersing himself so much into the match that he seemed to forget where he was. The crowd would remind him with their regular chants of "Harris! Harris!" as he galloped after the ball.

In an epic match with Slovakia, the game was tied at 5:5, resulting in a penalty shoot-out. Inevitably, the crowd demanded Harris take the kick. And sure enough, out he strolled to bang the ball into the net and win the game. Cue: mass celebration.

Team USA had passed their wildest expectations in terms of performance. Despite twice losing close matches to Sweden (who would top the section), they had the better of the others in the group and beat Slovakia, Spain and Switzerland to end up in second place. Slovakia would be third. And Spain? Well, despite having been helped by Real Madrid and having had Ronaldo take one of their training sessions, they were to stumble and disappoint. Fourth place was as good as they could manage.

Group C was to prove a canter for England. Denmark and Ireland offered little opposition, and while the Russians were to provide tougher games, there seemed to be no stopping the English. The squad had been selected through a process created by an organisation called the Street League founded by Dr. Damian Hatton, who worked in association with *The Big Issue in the North*.

The Street League had been founded in London and sought to involve homeless people, refugees, asylum seekers and anyone who considered themselves to be excluded from society. The key to the success of the England squad, however, was the involvement of Manchester United. Homeless players were selected from different areas of the country and were taken to United's famous Carrington training ground for coaching and selection. Rumour has it that Sir Alex Ferguson was to pick the final English squad. Though this has never been substantiated, it has now become an important story in Homeless World Cup folklore.

In addition to being supplied with the best training facilities in the land, the English squad were also to have two of United's full-time professional coaches by their side. They came with the team to Graz, staying for the whole competition and making a significant impact on the performance of the English team. Their early success in Group C had them quckly marked down as one of the favourites alongside the Dutch.

Every team was to bring their own colour and special individuality to the event. The Danish brought a group of fans who chanted, "We are red, we are white, we are Danish dynamite," throughout every match. Pele had dropped in during their preparations in Denmark and his magic seemed to rub off, with the team qualifying in second place, although this was only on goal difference. The Russians were to prove the most erratic side in the competition, exemplified by Maksim Mastitsky. He was one of the tournament's most outstanding players, yet was tempestuous and was to receive a number of blue cards, leaving his team exposed. This showed in their performances, results and final group placing of third, one place above the unfortunate Irish who were to fall in each of the matches. Scotland were involved in Group D and, as seems traditional, the section was quickly renamed the 'Group of Death'. It contained a further four teams – Brazil, Austria, Italy, and Poland, and it soon became evident that all of the sides within this group had the potential to win the tournament.

The opening games were the most anticipated. Not only was the host nation taking part but the Brazilians were about to make their entrance. With victories in their opening games, both sides met as evening fell. In front of an adoring home crowd, the Austrians managed a 1:1 draw, before winning a heart-stopping penalty shoot-out 4:3.

The closeness of the group meant that teams were taking points off one another and the section hung in the balance. While Scotland lost agonisingly to Brazil, they overcame Austria 2:1 and defeated Poland 5:3 to remain in sight of qualification. But on the second day of games, they failed to live up to expectations and were to suffer a series of demoralising defeats.

No doubt this was due in part to the previous evening's expeditions around the bars of Graz with the Irish squad.

In the end, Brazil were to top the group, followed closely by Austria and Italy. Add in England and Holland, and most spectators believed it was from these teams that we would find the eventual winners. Graz was beginning to dream of a host nation victory.

7

"So, that will be homeless people, then"

The Homeless World Cup had reached its halfway stage and was proving to be a much bigger event than we had antici-pated. Granted, the media had always been interested in the story and the opening press conference on the first day was well attended. But rather than subside, the attention on the tournament was ever-growing. As agency journalists filed their copy, newspapers began to pick up on what was going on and writers were dispatched to Graz.

We agreed that the media could have free access to the entire event including the players – as long as they respected the privacy of the participants when it was asked for. The combi-nation of football and the very real human stories surrounding the players was a heady one for newspapers. And ripe for abuse and intrusion. Thankfully, the journalists understood the concerns and our relationship throughout the tournament was excellent.

In the morning prior to the games, Harald and I would face the expanding media throng. Ninety journalists had been accredited at the media centre but many more had just turned up and we were soon to be conducting interviews at all times of the day and night. The story was hitting the front pages of many European newspapers, such as the famous Italian sports daily, *La Gazzetta dello Sport*, and naturally, there was huge interest from the Austrian media who followed events in much detail.

We also had enquiries from many countries who were not taking part, such as South Korea, Australia, Japan, Kenya, Colombia and Canada. Layla Mathers, who had left her job with INSP a few months before the event began, sent an e-mail to inform us that the tournament had been featured on the front page of the main daily paper in Tanzania.

In addition, there seemed to be a swarm of television and film crews. *The New York Times* had run a story about Team USA in the lead-up to the tournament, with the result that HBO and ESPN were in Graz to capture events. We had become used to two television people turning up when they wanted to run a story, one with the camera and the other doing the interviewing, but the Americans had brought full crews with them to cover all eventualities. Naturally, they were to concentrate on Team USA but they took hours of footage and their professionalism was above reproach. The HBO documentary came out in the US during the latter half of 2003 to great acclaim. They had managed to capture the story without being overdramatic or sentimental.

A number of teams had also been accompanied by documentary makers, such as the famous Polish director Mirek Dembinski. He had followed a number of squads – Poland, England, Russia, Brazil, South Africa and USA – in the build-up to the finals and was now integrating this material with the story currently unfolding. His film was released shortly after the 2003 Homeless World Cup was complete. It is titled *Losers and Winners* and offers a fine insight and reflection on what happened in Graz.

And it wasn't just the media who were being carried along by the excitement of it all. The crowds coming to watch the games had been growing steadily and their enjoyment was obvious. People who loved sport were relishing the excitement of the competition, especially having witnessed Austria being involved in a pulsating qualifying section.

But it was not just a football tournament. The circumstances of the players added a special dimension that appeared to connect with the spectators. They cheered, no matter what country the player came from, and no matter how brilliant or poor at football they happened to be.

There was an evening when Harald and I were standing by the main arena when we became aware of a commotion on the streets nearby. The Dutch squad were approaching and people who had been sitting at cafés had risen to their feet and had begun applauding. There were children running up to the players and demanding that they sign autographs, and the team was being followed by a band of supporters. It was a remarkable sight.

Harald and I looked at each other.

"So, that will be homeless people, then," we said in unison.

A transformation was taking place. A week previously, and these very same people would have been reviled, spat upon and often assaulted for no other reason than for being homeless. They are slammed by politicians and media commentators, who blame them for the many ills of city life, and demand that homeless people be removed as they are littering our streets and turning away potential tourists.

What was going on? The answer was simple and provides the basis for solutions throughout the world. The important point to remember is that the people have not changed. But the landscape had. The challenge, if we are to end homelessness and tackle poverty, is for us to create a different environment.

This must also include changing our own introverted attitudes. The residents of Graz were spectating in growing numbers because they could sense something of great value was unfolding.

With all this attention, we could only hope that the football would live up to its billing.

8

*"They were to concede 65 goals in the group,
while only netting once, for which they received
a massive cheer"*

In most international tournaments, the top two teams from each group would qualify for the second stage and the others would be journeying home. This, however, was not the case at the Homeless World Cup. After the opening stage, we created two tiers of competition with the winning teams going through to one, while the other sides participated in another. We were trying to create a system where teams gradually found their own level and in which, come the last day, everyone would be playing in what could be termed their "cup final".

The upper section of teams were split into two groups of five and were to play each other once. In Group 1, Holland swept through, destroying Sweden 8:1, Slovakia 21:0, Denmark 7:4 and Austria 4:2. With full points from all games, the odds were being shortened on the Dutch becoming the Homeless World Cup Champions.

Austria were to join Holland in the semi-finals, following victories over Denmark 9:1, Sweden 5:0 and Slovakia 21:0. There was some disquiet over the margin of victory in this latter match, the crowd feeling that the result was not in the spirit of the competition. The Austrian team, however, had no wish to humiliate the Slovakians, but their qualification was dependent upon goal difference. They had to keep scoring. In the end, Slovakia were to concede 65 goals in the group, while only netting once, for which they received a massive cheer.

Group 2 saw the Brazilians top the section, though not without difficulties. They may have dismantled the much-talked about English side 6:0, but they were to suffer a loss to South Africa. However, Brazil regained their poise with a 15:0 thrashing of the US before ekeing out a 3-2 win against the improving Italians.

They were to be joined in the semi-finals by England, who recovered from their opening loss to defeat South Africa, USA and, in a dramatic style, Italy. With a lead of 4-2, the Italians decided to try and hold the ball as the clock ticked down. However, with thirty seconds remaining, they conceded a goal and with renewed vigour the English continued to harry and press their opposition. It came down to the final two seconds. On the edge of their own area, the Italians dithered. There was no hesitation from the English and the match was all-square. Penalties ensued and England triumphed 2:1. The Italians had snatched defeat from the jaws of victory.

Team USA was also to suffer losses: five out of five. Ultimately, however, they had been thrilled at their progress.

"To win one game was just so great for us but to come here and actually qualify for the upper section and play against teams like Brazil and Italy was beyond our wildest dreams," explained Ron Grunberg, the American manager.

As the Homeless World Cup had been progressing, the lower section action had been doing likewise. Teams were divided into two groups of four with the INSP Networking trophy for the winners.

Poland romped away with Group 1, emerging with three wins over Ireland 6:4, Spain 15:0 and Wales 9:1. The Irish finished second, while the Welsh lost all three of their encounters.

Scotland, meanwhile, still smarting over the embarrassing manner of their elimination from the main trophy, won Group 2 convincingly by defeating Russia 7:2, Switzerland 13:0 and Germany 10:1. The Russians finished second while the Swiss once more finished with without a victory. But they did manage to net four times against Russia, each goal receiving a standing ovation.

Saturday was to prove finals day with each team having something to play for, even if it was just seventeenth place. An hour before the arena opened there were already queues. The television personnel ensured their cameras were in place and, back at the village, the coaches put their players through last minute preparations. By the end of the evening, we would know who were victorious in the inaugural Homeless World Cup.

The two top teams from the lower section were to compete for The INSP Networking Trophy. Scotland were desperate to atone for their earlier mishaps and having beaten Poland twice during the initial qualification, they were favourites to win. Of course, when a Scottish footballing side is involved, nothing is straightforward. And so it proved.

The game finished 2-2 and was to move into sudden death penalties. The nerves of all players showed, but it was goalkeeper Stewart Griffin that was to prove the hero with a magnificent save. The blue of Scotland was celebrating and in terms of overall position, they had finished 11th.

The first semi-final of the Homeless World Cup was to

feature Holland and England. Rain, however, was to delay the start as the surface was slippery and therefore hazardous. There was a long wait before weather conditions improved but when the football returned, it was of a high and dramatic standard.

England played some excellent possession football and the Dutch appeared to be taken aback. It was no surprise when the English took the lead. But just when it seemed they would hold on to their slender margin, the Dutch were awarded a penalty. Only seconds remained. Jeandro Baylin stepped up and finished with aplomb. Holland were on level terms but their concentration had been momentarily disrupted. With their goalkeeper still celebrating their equaliser, England broke away and slid home a winner with two seconds remaining. They thought it was all over . . . well, it was now. The Dutch were out.

With this result still reverberating around the stands, Brazil faced Austria in a game that was to end in tears. An enthralling match, soundtracked by a vociferous home support, it finished 1:1, which meant penalty kicks. And Austria proved successful. As they celebrated with the crowd, the Brazilian players began to cry. Their dream of returning home with the trophy had been shattered in the cruellest of ways. But they had been great favourites with the crowd and there was much applause for their efforts.

The scene, however, was set for an Austria-England final, not quite what had been forecast. As the two sides went off to rest, and the remaining other fixtures were to be completed, it began to rain once more. We were now seriously behind schedule and we had to contemplate postponement with the idea of returning the following morning. This would obviously have destroyed the atmosphere which had been created in the dramatic build-up to the final. If at all possible, we wanted to try and finish on Saturday evening. The crowd refused to move and waited patiently for the rain to stop.

Harald phoned the local airport to ask for a weather report. They confirmed it would stop raining. But would it be in time to save the competition? This simply added to the tension and drama that surrounded the evening. There was nothing we could do but wait for the clouds to lift.

9

*"I will never try suicide again . . . because I
now know that whatever happens I will always
retain my self-respect"*

During the break for the inclement weather, I took the opportunity to talk to the Manchester United coaches Dave Bell and
Louis Garvey, who had been looking after the England squad.
They maintained that the best football sides in the world were
not necessarily made up of the finest possible talent. It was their
belief that teamwork was the key to success and that you had to
be the type of individual that could participate and learn from
others. Otherwise, and regardless of your skills, you would not
break into a side such as Man Utd.

The challenge was to develop the individual into a team
player, whilst retaining their unique skills. This was a key
psychological aspect to every footballer and they believed the
same applied to homeless people.

"You've got to take the homelessness out of people's heads
as much as anything and you can do that by involving them in
teams," they said.

You could see this influence on the current England squad.
The players had grown in confidence during the tournament

and they had developed a self-belief which had propelled them into the final. In fact, this had happened to most of the players. Their confidence and self-esteem had grown with every day and time and again, players from differing countries were to tell me how they were never going back to where they had come from.

One of the players, who wished to remain nameless, informed me that only a short time earlier he had tried to commit suicide following the separation from his family. He had ended up homeless and in despair, with depression and a feeling of worthlessness soon following.

"Now I am here and I've never experienced anything like this, so I will go back home and I can promise you I will never try suicide again in my life, because I now know that whatever happens I will always retain my self-respect. It's down to these people in Graz who applauded and spoke to me and made me feel human."

The clouds were indeed lifting.

The cameraman covering the tournament for Reuters television was worried about his time slots. But he was determined to hang on. As we talked, he told me how much he was enjoying the competition and explained how the openness of everybody was appreciated.

"At the big matches, you have to wade through agents and rules just to speak to a player, but what you have here is more about what football should be all about," he said.

"The thing is, as soon as these matches start, you totally forget that the players are in fact homeless."

And this is what it was all about – creating lasting change and removing the stigma of homelessness. At the same time, and crucially linked, it was about the power to help everyone else, such as him, to see the potential of all people, allowing us to create mechanisms and platforms which benefit all society.

The rain was off and the football was back on. The fans had stayed and they watched the remaining matches with fervour, including Holland's comfortable 4:1 victory over Brazil to clinch third place. And then we were ready for the final match of the tournament.

The home crowd roared for their favourites as they battled against a well-organised England team. In a highly-entertaining and close-fought match, the locals had their way, as the hosts gained the upper-hand to claim a 2:1 win: Austria had won the 2003 Homeless World Cup!

At the closing ceremony, every player was given the same medal while being presented with a different cup to signify the position in which they had finished. The crowd cheered and applauded every presentation. There were two special trophies – one for the top scorer which was handed to Slataru Birinell of Italy, and a Fair Play award. Each of the team coaches had been asked to vote, and they were unanimous in their selection. The Swiss team were overcome with joy.

And then the Austrians were presented with the Homeless World Cup. The trophy was held aloft and all of the teams started to dance in the centre of the arena. Everyone went on an impromptu lap of honour to the sound of 'We are the Champions' and a mass of of footballers from all over the world joined hands, hugged and celebrated a week which had given the world something special. The flashlights popped and the television cameras whirred as the media captured the moment for the rest of the world to see. And in the background, the spectators joined in as well: clapping, dancing and refusing to go home.

Street soccer folklore will repeat that the whole world shook at the moment and that something changed forever. There is nothing wrong with hyperbole on such an occasion. And anyway, I'd like to think it was true. It was a privilege to witness such scenes. The Homeless World Cup had been an unforgettable triumph.

The celebrations were to move from the city centre back to the players' village. Participants from rival teams mixed together, unable to speak the same language but perfectly capable of understanding each other. And all too soon it was time for goodbye. Souvenirs and contact numbers were exchanged and the guides that had been attached to each team, providing information and making sure they got to the games on time, said their farewells also.

Everyone was to leave with fond memories of Graz – of its people and its picturesque land. But this, we told ourselves, was only a beginning. The Homeless World Cup should become a regular event and the biggest driving factor was the post-competition results which seemed to indicate that most of the players had gone back to their own country and moved away from homelessness. Our main objective had been achieved. We had proved that sport could provide the basis for social integration. There was no doubt in my mind, therefore, that we had to try and expand upon these initial successes. It had worked. And people's lives had changed.

10

*"A child cannot live on the streets . . . I want
to show that I am a good father"*

His name is Modesto. It may mean 'modest' yet it is his
innocence that is most apparent. He remains a believer in
people and trusts in a better tomorrow. It is unusual to hear
such sentiments from a man who has spent over five years
living on the streets.

"Bad luck and a bad head," he replies, when asked how he
became homeless. "I had some problems with gambling and
my head can bring me bad ideas. I didn't want to be kidnapped
by them anymore."

Football was to provide the necessary diversion, and Modesto was to represent Spain in the 2003 Homeless World Cup.
It was a magical experience and he is keen to share his
enthusiasm and encourage other homeless people to train
towards it.

"The tournament was so important for me, that I now feel a
debt to it. I am supporting the organisers, and the players, and
I will do everything I can to help. I am sure my own experience
will be of real value and I want to share it."

Modesto had lived in the centre of Madrid with five dogs

and a cat. There were no shelters, no rented houses and no hostels. But, he admits, there was a sense of freedom.

"And, in general, people were kind," he says. "They knew I wasn't a thief, and they trusted me. People would even ask me to take care of their market stalls and I felt I was part of the community, even if I didn't have a proper home. And although it is very hard to be homeless, I was able to get by. It was a peculiar life, very uncomfortable but not as dramatic as some people would make out."

Circumstances have since changed for Modesto. He is currently living in a hostel with his girlfriend and his son, who is two months old.

"A roof is needed for little David. We asked the authorities for an opportunity to take care of him. I understand that a child cannot live on the streets. We are doing everything, obeying every little rule, in order to stay with my son. I want to show that I am a good father."

When Modesto is asked whether taking part in the Homeless World Cup altered his attitude to life, his face immediately lights up. His answer is obvious.

"Let me tell you," he states. "When I returned from Graz, the police had taken all my possessions which I had hidden in the park. All I had in the world was the great feelings I brought back from Austria. They were of friendship. I could only speak Spanish and everyone else spoke their own language but, and I don't know how, we all managed to understand each other.

"I had never, in all my life, travelled out of Spain. I'd never even been on a plane and suddenly all my dreams were becoming true. They were coming true through football, something that I had always loved playing. For me, it was a wonderful meeting up with those in similar circumstances to me. I don't know how but I could follow what the other players were saying even if I couldn't recognise a single word.

There was a universal language: football. And just one spirit: to show the world that homeless people are not aliens."

When Modesto begins to talk about his experiences, it is often best simply to listen. He is captured by the memories and is eager to relate.

"Other teams looked so tall and strong. In contrast, we were quite short and some of us looked very weak. But we were not. We'd had too many hard experiences to be as weak as we looked. So, we needed to show people, and show ourselves, that we had been training hard.

"We didn't want to look like poor people who play football. No way. We were football players representing our country. We were footballers who, due to our circumstances, just happened to live on the street. David Beckham lives in a palace in Madrid and he plays football with other people who live in palaces but if his circumstances had been different he might have been playing in the Homeless World Cup. Where you happen to live is no indicator about how you might play.

"Unfortunately in Graz, we didn't play as well as I would have liked. We were trying to think why that was and concluded that we were very nervous when we went onto the court. We wanted to show many things; possibly we were trying too hard and it was difficult to free ourselves, enjoy the game and just play. We were captured by nerves and we vowed that next time this would not happen.

"I have a great many memories about the training also. We worked hard, and we learnt how to work, not just for your own self, but for the whole team. It was so important because we were responsible for the development of everyone. We knew anything was possible if we focussed all our energy together.

"And as soon as we arrived at Graz, I was so happy. People

were really warm. You could feel a special atmosphere. We were living something *special*. And we knew that. A few days ago I watched a video of the Graz championship. It brought back many very special memories and it underlined to me that I had to take advantage of every opportunity life handed me. The Homeless Word Cup was such an opportunity. It was a once-in-a-lifetime experience and when these things come along it is important to make the most of them because they show you that you can achieve things you never imagined were possible."

Modesto's eyes glow with pride and he laughs a little.

"Well, this is a little embarrassing to say but the team had a motto. In the first days we used to say: 'Why are we here? In order to get the Cup. And if we don't win it? We will steal it.' But after sharing our time with the other teams and organisers we decided to change it. 'Why are we here? In order to get the Cup. And if we don't win it? So, we buy it.' It sounds much better, doesn't it?

"You just feel such a special person when you go out onto the court. Oh!!!! Hundreds of people are shouting nice things at you, demanding that you score a goal. You just feel this huge wave of support for you. Support me – a homeless man who lives in Madrid? But the most incredible thing of all, as the finals approached, people would stop me in the street, shake my hand really strongly and ask for my autograph. I just couldn't believe it. Me?

"The whole atmosphere in Graz was just incredible – I remember the barbeques, songs, music, fires, unforgettable. Real life is easier when you have such memories."

Now, Modesto manages to get work one day at a time. He seeks regular employment to give his child security and stability.

"I want to be like everyone else," he says. "And keep my

family together. I want my child to be proud of me. To see me as a winner, at least, a man who has travelled around the world because he is not the man who looks for garbage. To see me as a footballer who has represented his country and a man who works for his dreams. I want to feel as though I'm alive. I mean, I'm a human being after all, that's what counts isn't it? And we all have goals to reach."

Modesto was talking to Monica Sanchez, who worked as a journalist for Madrid's street newspaper Milhistorias. *Talking to Modesto is always a pleasure, she says, even if it usually means rushing along beside him, as he hurriedly makes his way to football training.*

11

*"Homeless people need soccer for the same
reason that everyone else needs it"*

St. Petersburg is a dream city. Its stunning architecture and rich
history merge together to provide a backdrop that is always
inspiring and often uplifting. Unless, that is, you happen to be
homeless.

The number of unemployed and homeless people in Russia
is impossible to quantify. All that is known is that it is ever-
growing and substantial, regardless of what the authorities
might like to think.

Arkady Tiurin runs the street paper in St. Petersburg called
Put Domoi, which translates to 'Journey Home'. The publication has walked along an uneven path since it was launched,
often feeling the financial strains. A determined Arkady,
however, has stuck with it. And he was to become the manager
of the Russian squad that arrived in Graz.

"Homeless people need soccer for the same reason that
everyone else needs it," he comments. "It is a wonderful
method of enjoying life – enjoying it collectively, too."

The captain of Russia in 2003 was forty-two-year-old Yuri
Kuzmin.

"I became homeless in 1998 after the economic crisis which took place in August of that year," Yuri explained to Arkady. "I had my own business and I ran a footwear shop. But once the crisis hit, the sale of my flat became necessary.

"I tried not to think about being homeless. Life continued. I tried to find work and I still had my girlfriend. My friends were still around me. The only man who decided to leave me alone with my problems was my business partner.

"I was to hear about the Homeless World Cup when I happened to be watching television one day. Being an adventurer, I decided to try my strength. Anything new is always interesting and I began to play football for the first time in my life. It was quite traumatic but fascinating feeling and seeing what playing soccer could do.

"I was very proud to be selected. I was one of the first people to take part in this event – I was a discoverer and it was important to get acquainted with the players from other countries. I'll always remember the Swiss team. Those guys certainly knew how to feel and enjoy life. They had a big impact.

"But the strongest impression was left by a small orchestra from Latin America. They were playing on a nearby stage between games. Suddenly, the lead musician, announced, 'This next song will be played for the Russian team'. He had studied in St. Petersburg some years before. The team tried to hide our tears. I will never forget this moment.

"The arena was full of spectators. We were supported, not only by Russians who happened to be in Graz, but many other people who were watching. It felt good to be appreciated."

12

"We destroyed the stereotype – we didn't look homeless, we were proud, we looked smart and the people watching thought we were cool. And we were"

"I was a victim of 9/11," he states, when he explains how he became homeless.

The building Rory Levine worked in, adjacent to the Twin Towers, was blown to smithereens during the attack. Fate played its part. He was late for work. If Rory had been on time . . .

"Thanks be to God," he says.

While his life was spared, Rory's job was gone. With no income he couldn't pay the rent and the landlord threw him out. He received compensation for his situation as a result of 9/11 but the payment came through too late to save his tenancy and he ended up on the streets. As the world grieved for the victims and families of the tragedy, Rory, like the thousands of other homeless people, was simply forgotten. To all extents, he had become invisible.

Rory arrived at the Grand Central Neighborhood Social Services Corporation which runs a variety of programmes through its Mainchance scheme. It provides basic shelter in the form of lounge chairs in an overnight seating area, right through to integrated employment and housing programmes.

The philosophy of Mainchance is based on what they say is "consumerism rather than paternalism". They let the homeless people decide what kind of help they want. A framework is then provided which supports them through their own efforts. Many of the staff are formerly homeless, providing proof to new arrivals of what is possible.

The project has two publications: *Upward*, which is written by homeless people for homeless people and distributed around New York's shelters, and *Big News* which is sold by vendors as a means of employment and income.

Big News had started in April 2000 and now sells around 15,000 copies a month. As a delegate to the INSP conferences, Ron Grunberg, the editor of the paper, found the notion of a street soccer tournament involving homeless people as "ridiculous" and "frankly amazing".

"Obviously, the Europeans knew what this was all about and seemed enthusiastic, so I threw my hand in but I just couldn't imagine it," he said.

"There was a lot of discussion and one or two heated moments, particularly when the issue of women playing was discussed, but there were people who were determined to make it happen. I remember causing laughter when I asked if the players should wear hard hats. I thought it was a sensible enough question at the time!"

Despite his doubts, Ron set about organising training sessions and recruiting players. To begin with they organised training once a week at 1pm before their writing group, which started two hours later.

"I heard about it through Ron and I thought, why not, let's give it a try," explains Rory. "I'd played some soccer at high school and I was okay, I guess, and I just wanted to be involved in something.

"We didn't really know what we were doing to start with," admits Ron. "But we were determined and Stephanie, who was attached to our project, took the day off once a week to become our coach. We'd just go down to the training park and see who would turn up. One time, no-one did. Graz seemed a long way off."

But slowly more homeless people came along and a nucleus of regulars was to keep the momentum going.

Fund raising was another challenge but Ron's incredulity that the event was ever going to take place, let alone with a USA team involved, was starting to wane when funds to cover flights were confirmed through international sponsorship.

"We had new challenges to face and many of our players just couldn't make it out of the country due to identification and visa related issues," explains Ron. "One player had problems with child support payment arrears, for example, and he couldn't get the papers which allowed him to get a passport."

Despite all these obstacles, the USA team of 9 players, one coach and one manager, accompanied by a horde of enthusiastic media people, crossed the Atlantic bound for Austria.

Graz made an immediate impression upon Rory. It was clean, quiet and people "seemed to drink beer quite freely". They settled quickly into their accommodation and made friends with their immediate neighbours from Brazil, South Africa and Ireland.

"We won our first game and I felt overwhelmed," recalls Rory. "It was exhilarating. People were actually cheering us. The media was following us, their cameras were flashing and their microphones were pushed towards us."

Rory became popular with the crowds with his trademark high-five and bandana.

"Yes, the kids started wearing bandanas which was cool. I had this toothpick and after a couple of days I noticed these kids with toothpicks as well. I'd become a bit of a trend setter over there. I really warmed to the crowd and it was reciprocated.

"We destroyed the stereotype of the homeless person – we didn't look homeless, we were proud, we looked smart and the people watching thought we were cool. And we were. We were athletes.

"The tournament gave me a new perspective. After Graz, I thought 'I can beat this homeless thing'. I might have returned to where I was, to the shelter, but in my mind, I was now just passing through."

Rory moved out of the shelter eventually and now has a full-time job as a messenger and lives together with his god-sister in the Bronx. Ron, meanwhile, still finds difficulty in expressing his experience of Graz.

"To talk just about the soccer doesn't do it justice. For me, it was a transporting moment. It was unimaginable and unforgettable. It's like an intervention or a moment in time. I remember I read about a man in Thailand who was driving along and his arm was ripped off at some traffic lights. He drove for 75 miles before he noticed. It's absurd but I always remember this rather than the book. That's what the Homeless World Cup was like.

"Some people say it was a waste of money and the cash should have been used to feed people. Man doesn't live by bread alone, however. Sitting eating soup three times a day is mind-numbingly boring but you can change through some form of active engagement and that's what happened with the Homeless World Cup in Graz."

It is likely that both Ron and Rory will be featured in a major movie being made for the cinema about the Homeless World Cup. They've signed individual contracts and the script for the film is currently being written.

"It's a little unbelievable but, hey," says Rory. "That's life and this film thing is kind of cool."

"And what actor should play you?" I ask.

There's a pause.

"Omar Epps, yeah, Omar Epps would work," he says eventually, half-laughing.

"And what about Ron, who do you think should play Ron?"

"Albert Brooks."

The Rory and Ron Story – coming to a cinema near you soon.

13

"They feared that upon arrival, they would 'disappear' and attempt to remain in the country"

In the aftermath of Graz, we established a small non-profit-making company which we called ProPoor Sports Ltd. Harald Schmied, Bernhard Wolf (who had taken over the organisation in Graz in the months leading up to the event) and I became its first directors. Our job was to ensure the successful promotion of the Homeless World Cup and to secure its long-term future.

It was felt that the tournament would benefit greatly from being moved around the world. Not only would it become a special event for the host city but it would broaden the minds of all involved, including the players, and build upon the concept of family and community. In addition, Harald correctly pointed out that the Graz event had gone ahead because the city had been chosen as the European City of Culture and there had been an existing infrastructure to support the event. Without that, it would difficult for the city to host the tournament again. Thus, we decided to seek a new venue for 2004.

A bidding process was organised amongst the members of the International Network of Street Papers (INSP), much like the procedure countries became involved in when they are looking to host the Olympic Games. We asked that the potential bidders consider their own internal capacity, think about what support they could get from their city and country, and what potential sponsorship would be available.

The successful bid came from the Swedish street paper, *Faktum*, which was based in Gothenburg. They were very enthusiastic and everyone had been impressed by their organisation, both on the football side and with their players when they had been in Austria. The city also had vast experience with hosting major international football and sporting events. Each July it played host to the Gotha Cup, a huge youth soccer competition involving hundreds of teams from across the globe. The Homeless World Cup, we thought, would present little problem.

As with the Austrian event, we split the organising into two distinct parts. *Faktum* at the Swedish end would look after all the local matters, including sponsorship, while we would take care of international fundraising and ensuring the teams would be able to travel to and from Gothenburg.

With the wider publicity from Graz and the excitement within the street paper movement, it was inevitable that more teams would want to take part. The number was increased to 26, with the additional squads coming from Namibia, Argentina, Japan, Ukraine, Portugal, France, Canada and the Czech Republic.

Two other teams almost made it. The Kenyan side were late with their visas applications, while the Cameroon squad were denied entry into the country by the Swedish authorities. All documentation had been completed and filed as required, the players met the eligibility criteria and each possessed a passport. Despite our interventions and repeated assurances, the Swedish Government failed to budge. They feared that upon arrival, the Cameroonians would 'disappear' and attempt to remain in the country, citing a previous experience with a team of Cameroon youngsters.

It didn't matter that we knew the project behind this team, and that it had been recognised by various world organisations. We also alluded to the previous year's events in Graz and the exemplary report given to us by the Austrian authorities. No one seemed to listen, however. And the Cameroon squad was refused the right to participate in the Homeless World Cup.

There was anger and upset. The team had done everything that was asked of them but it was of no consequence. What was the point in creating systems for people to adhere to if you are just going to ignore them and make indiscriminate decisions anyway?

I was still furious when I arrived at Gothenburg, ahead of the opening ceremony. The pre-tournament press conference was dominated by questions about the incident, but I did not want it to dominate the event. There were 26 teams involved and we needed to celebrate their participation. The absence of our friends in Cameroon, however, would not be forgotten.

The tournament would follow a similar format to that of Graz, from the opening ceremony where the players marched from their 'village', through the streets of Gothenburg and on to the Götenplatzen in the city centre where we had erected a street soccer arena. The Swedish crowd cheered as each nation appeared.

Speeches from Carina Lindberg, chairman of *Factum*, and by Michael Kleiner of the United Nations set the context for the week ahead. The spirit of Gothenburg was alive and the second Homeless World Cup was soon to be underway.

The teams were split into eight groups, playing each other once, with eight teams having been seeded following their performances in Graz. The World Champions Austria looked on imperious form, crushing Canada 11:1 before going on to win their section. This would also include a 10:4 victory over Japan, a squad made up of older players, many of whom appeared to be playing football for the first time. When they arrived on court, the team would bow and wave to the crowd and very quickly became the team that everyone loved.

Austria were to be joined in the next stage by Canada, who were making their tournament debut. They would be joined by their North American neighbours when the USA defeated Portugal 6:3 to emerge from their section as the second-placed qualifier. The group would be topped by England, who struggled to a 4:3 win against Team USA. This would follow on from a narrow 3:2 victory over Portugal. The English professional side had lost to their Portuguese counterparts on penalties during the UEFA European Championship earlier in the summer and the English squad in Gothenburg felt that this result gave them "sweet revenge". The Portuguese begged to differ.

Group C was to prove too much for Ireland.

"The draw was terrible for us," mused their enthusiastic coach, Mike Pender. "We're much better than some of the other teams who have qualified from the other sections, but that's football, I guess.

"We played really well against two excellent teams, Poland and Holland, who will both be there at the death but we'll pick ourselves up and our aim is now to win the Networking Trophy."

The Scottish team, however, have little difficulty in negotiating their group. They hadn't been seeded but they were to complete straightforward victories over Slovakia 8:0, Czech Republic 6:2 and, surprisingly, 9:2 against Brazil. This last result automatically increased the expectations on the Scottish team. Their media quickly turned the players into heroes, as the nation had never beaten Brazil at any footballing level. Anticipation was growing – was the Scottish team in Gothenburg about to change years of failure and return home with the trophy . . . ?

Brazil were to qualify in second place, despite another defeat at the hands of the Czech Republic. The Czechs were unable to beat Slovakia and, therefore, with their near-neighbours, they headed into the Networking Trophy section.

Argentina and, more impressively, Italy were to emerge from Section E, which also contained Switzerland and Namibia. The Swiss had undoubtedly improved from the previous year and were scoring goals and competing well. The Namibians were one of the tournament's new boys, and a bond was quickly to develop between the two squads. It didn't matter that Namibia were to defeat Switzerland 11:7, both sides continued to mix together during their free time.

The Namibians were clearly in awe of the Western city. They'd never seen or experienced anything like it and couldn't believe how expensive everything was. The Swiss took the squad under their wing. They were able to exchange experiences and learn about contrasting lives. This dimension, which infiltrates the competition from the moment the event kicks off, is often described as the Spirit of the Homeless World Cup.

Group F was a thrilling section involving Spain, Ukraine and Denmark where each team won one match, thereby gaining three points. It came down to goal difference and the Spanish, by the margin of one goal, were to lose out.

Russia had improved considerably since the previous event and were to win Group G with victories over France and South Africa. The latter were to join them in qualification having scraped a 3:2 victory over the French.

The hosts were to be found in the final section and were to

play their games in front of a packed and naturally vociferous crowd. A 7:3 defeat of Germany was followed by overcoming Wales 5:1. The Welsh, however, were to recover and a 4:1 win over Germany saw them book their place in the upper tier of round two. Just as in Graz, the Homeless World Cup was proving once more to be an exciting and riveting competition. And it was also noticeable how the standard of football was improving. It meant that any number of teams were in the running for the ultimate prize.

14

"I'm over the moon . . . they deserve to celebrate as much as they like"

It seemed easier to understand while actually at the tournament than it does to write down now. Basically, the sixteen qualifying teams would go on to play in four groups of four, playing each other once. The top two from each group would go on to play for the main trophy, the Homeless World Cup. The bottom two sides from each section would fall into the intermediate cup, the Factum Trophy.

The ten teams that failed in qualifying from the opening stage would play for the ISNP Networking Trophy, divided into two groups of five, playing each other twice. One section was named Golden Goal, while the other was called Street Spirit.

Golden Goal was dominated by the Irish. They won all of their eight games against Japan, the Czech Republic, France and Namibia. It possibly proved Mike Pender's earlier assertion that they'd been eliminated from a very strong qualifying group. The team was now being backed by some very enthusiastic supporters who provided colourful vocal backing and were almost to merge into being part of the actual team.

Namibia finished in second place, winning six out of their eight matches, while endearing themselves to the crowd. The French finished third, followed by the Czech Republic and the Japanese. Although they lost every match, Japan managed to score twenty-six goals and twenty-six loud cheers were heard across Gothenburg.

The Street Spirit grouping was to feature Switzerland, Germany, Portugal, Spain and Slovakia. The section was to be dominated by the Iberian neighbours with Portugal sneaking out on top. Spain would have expected at least to be level on points with the Portuguese having defeated them once, but a surprise defeat at the hands of Germany proved their undoing.

By the end of the section, the Germans came in third having won three of their games, while the Swiss edged out Slovakia on goal difference. Their 9:8 victory over Switzerland had to be one of the ties of the round. The game started aggressively, though this was to melt as the goals flew in and the crowd's enthusiasm filtered around the arena.

The two groups in the Networking Trophy had been played in a real spirit of fair play, something which was greatly appreciated by the people who were watching. The position of 9th and 10th (or 25th and 26th overall) was to involve Japan and Slovakia. Again, this was a fantastic match, finishing 3:3, though many observers believe the Slovakians slowed their game right down and allowed their opponents to score. This has been denied but those watching have different opinions.

Japan were to win the penalty shoot-out and the crowd leapt to their feet. The scenes of jubilation continued and it was hard to get the Japanese players to leave the court in order to allow the next game to begin.

In the semi-finals of the INSP Networking Trophy, Ireland

claimed a dramatic 4:3 victory over Spain. With their green-clad supporters in the background, complete with an inflatable hammer which read: "Hammered by the Irish", they made for imposing opposition. In the second semi-final Portugal also had a narrow 2:1 victory, scraping past a Namibian team which had grown in confidence as the week progressed.

The Irish support, however, were now at fever pitch as their beloved team and Portugal walked out to the centre of the arena. They were to enter dreamland fifteen minutes later when their team overpowered the Portuguese 9:2.

"I'm over the moon. It's magnificent and full credit to the guys," said the fired-up Ireland coach Mike Pender after the match. "They deserve to celebrate as much as they like."

And they did.

Elsewhere, sixteen teams were competing for the Homeless World Cup. In the first group, Austria continued to dominate and the team was already beginning to look like favourites to retain the trophy. They won all their three matches and were too strong for Italy (5:0), Wales (6:0) and Brazil (9:3). Austria would be joined in qualification by Italy who were victorious in their remaining fixtures.

Group 2 proved a much closer affair. At one point any of the four teams could have qualified. In the end, South Africa proved successful. The runners-up spot would be decided in the final match between England and Holland. In yet another match of high quality, it ended 5:5 and we were once again treated to a penalty shoot-out. The English team held their nerve and Holland, one of the pre-tournament favourites, had exited at the hands of England for the second time running.

Russia, Poland, Ukraine and the USA competed in a section that was marked by the referee producing seven blue cards during one game, the most ever seen in the Homeless World Cup. The Russians came out victors 3:2 over Team USA, and were to progress onto the next stage, although only as runners-up. Top spot went to Poland who managed to pip the USA 6:4.

In Group 4, Scotland continued with their rich vein of form, emerging with three straight wins. It was, however, not without controversy. The match against Argentina provided the talking point. The Argentinians claimed that one of Scotland's goals had been mistakenly double-counted. Thus, what was truly a 3-3 draw, was credited to the Scots as 4-3. A documentary film crew from Argentina who had filmed the entire match seemed to confirm the tie, but the referee stuck with his original decision.

With Scotland already through to the next stage, and Canada's exit confirmed, the final qualification place rested on the outcome of the last match between the hosts Sweden and Argentina. Whoever won this game would go through. It was as simple as that. Once again, the stands were packed with fans and in a pulsating atmosphere, the hosts came out 5:3 winners.

The eight teams competing for the Faktum Trophy were split into two groups of four teams each, who were to play each other twice. The first group was called Hat Trick and involved Denmark, Canada, Wales and USA.

The Danes were to win all of their six games, while the Welsh and the Americans both finished with nine points each. Wales, however, had the superior goal difference. The Canadians, meanwhile, were the group whipping boys, suffering six losses and conceding 85 goals.

The second group, Team Spirit included Argentina, Brazil, Ukraine and Holland. Like Denmark, the Ukraine won six and were followed by Holland. The South American giants contested third place, with Argentina triumphing twice.

In the semi-finals, Denmark managed to squeeze past the Dutch 2:1, while the Welsh were held to a 2:2 draw by

Ukraine, before losing out on penalties. The final would also be settled in this manner and it was the Danes that were to taste sweet victory. The Red & White Army exploded with delight and their players danced alongside the beaten Ukrainians. The Faktum Trophy had its winner – congratulations Denmark.

2003. The Danish Coach meets Pele at the Danish national qualifying tournament. (Courtesy of www.hustorbi.ak)

2003. Ronaldo drops in to support the Spanish team. (Courtesy of www.wilhistorias.org)

Graz. Holland beat Wales 9:0. (Courtesy of Arie Kievit)

Graz. Super cool. The USA goalkeeper Rory Levine was very popular with the crowd.
(Courtesy of Arie Kievit)

Graz: The opening procession. Germany (left) and Spain (right) march into the stadium.
(Courtesy of Harry Schiffer)

Graz. Comrades in arms – the spirit between the teams was fantastic.
(Courtesy of Maurico Bustamante)

Graz. Peace. Switzerland won the Fair Play Award. (Courtesy of Harry Schiffer)

Graz. Thumbs up for friendship. (Courtesy of Harry Schiffer)

Graz. Goal – USA's Harris Pankin scores against Slovakia.

Graz. Sweden chase the ball against Spain.

Graz. My ball – Italy and Poland
close encounter in group D.

Graz. It's all over – the teams celebrate together.

Graz. All for glory. Brazilian colour and style added sparkle to the occasion.
(Courtesy of Arie Kievit)

The pictures on the next 4 pages are taken by Miguel Martriena. Miguel, an Argentinean, is an internationally renowned photographer who ended up becoming homeless himself. He arrived in Gothenburg and took hundreds of pictures including these portraits which capture the atmosphere of the tournament.

Gothenburg. The international spirit of the tournament captivated everyone.
(Courtesy of Mark Shipperlee)

Gothenburg. England's Kevin Wilson, won the best goalkeeper award.
(Courtesy of Gubisch/Lassacher)

Gothenburg. It's a goal – the standard of football was magnificent.
(Courtesy of Gubisch/Lassacher)

Gothenburg. The action was fast and exciting. (Courtesy of Mark Shipperlee)

Gothenburg. David Duke of Scotland dresses
for the occasion.
(Courtesy of Mark Shipperlee)

Gothenburg. The Austrians made it to the
final for the second year running.
(Courtesy of Gubisch / Lassacher)

Gothenburg. Where's the ball? The Dutch make it difficult for England.
(Courtesy of Mark Shipperlee)

Gothenburg. Will he score? There were many great goals and great saves.
(Courtesy of Mark Shipperlee)

Gothenburg. Ticker tape applause. The crowds loved the action.
(Courtesy of Gubisch/Lassacher)

Gothenburg. The teams gather together before the cup presentations.
(Courtesy of Mark Shipperlee)

Gothenburg. Japan, winners of the Fair Play Award. (Courtesy of Mark Shipperlee)

Gothenburg. Italy wins the second Homeless World Cup.
(Courtesy of Mark Shipperlee)

Gothenburg. The Co-founders. Harald Schmied (insert) and Mel Young (presenting the first Homeless World Cup).

15

*"A mound of bodies lay on the court,
surrounded by photographers and television
cameras"*

The draw had kept apart the only two unbeaten sides left in the
Homeless World Cup. But with plenty of other good teams in
the two groups, there was no guarantee that Austria and
Scotland would progress further.

In the first section, the UN group, Austria were drawn
together with Poland, England and Sweden and as ever football was to upset logic. In the opening match the Austrians
were unable to defeat England and in the ensuing penalties, the
English were to emerge victorious. The World Champions had
lost their opening game. But they were to recover and qualify
for the semi-finals. The hosts, however, failed miserably but
were still to play an important role in determining who would
continue alongside Austria.

In the final fixture, England were required to beat Sweden
by eleven goals. Although the Swedes had lost all of their
games and had suffered a previous 8:1 defeat at the hands of
the English, they were determined not to be rolled over. And so
it proved when the hosts opened the scoring. England quickly

restored order but the required result was simply too much. They may have won 12:4 but it was Poland who journeyed on to the next stage.

The UEFA group had Scotland, Italy, South Africa and Russia jousting for position. And it was the Italians who would find their form, waltzing through the group and winning all of their matches in style. The other sides took points from each other, resulting in the final fixture being the decider. Scotland had to defeat South Africa, otherwise the Russians would progress. In an exciting encounter, the Scots appeared nervous and were under the cosh for long periods of the game. With the match ending in a 3:3 draw, it all came down to penalty kicks. The Scottish goalkeeper held his nerve and his team were in the Homeless World Cup semi-finals.

Both matches were to be one-sided affairs, the Italians disposing of Poland 5:0, while the Austrians took care of Scotland 5:1. The Poles recovered from their disappointment better than the Scots and took third place with a 7:4 win. The scene was now set for the final. It appeared evenly matched, with the Italians playing well and knocking the ball about confidently. They had improved as the tournament progress and a 5:0 defeat by the Austrians earlier in the week appeared forgotten.

The consensus was that the two best teams had made it to the final. And the crowd anticipated a classic. Italy were to strike first. And then again. The Austrians appeared to lose their composure and their opponents readily seized the initiative. Two further goals and it was apparent that the trophy was heading towards Milan. As the final whistle blew, the Italians erupted in a magnificent display of joy. A mound of bodies lay on the court, surrounded by photographers and television cameras. The crowd saluted the new World Champions.

It had been a week of undoubted football brilliance. Japan

was awarded the Fair Play trophy and the top scorer was Yevgen Adamenko of the Ukraine who scored 53 goals in the tournament. Kevin Wilson of England received the best goalkeeper award for a string of match-winning performances. There was also a special mention for absent friends.

Prior to presenting the Homeless World Cup to the victorious Italian team, I was to say a few words of congratulations to the players. I told them that they were all heroes and had the right to stand proud. They had shown the world what could be done. I was then to ask everyone to provide a cheer which would carry across the night sky and be heard by the players left behind in Cameroon. It was an act of solidarity. Later than evening, the participants began to sign a T-shirt and a card. A package would be dispatched to Cameroon bearing these items and a number of other gifts supplied by the players. Homeless people knew what it was like to be excluded. It was something they had all experienced.

Once Italy stepped forward to receive their trophy, a mass celebration took place. All of the players, as in Graz, danced, hugged, shook hands and waved at the crowds. For the second year running, homeless people had shown the world just what can be done given the right opportunities. It had been a marvellous display of unity and friendliness and people's lives would be changed forever.

The spirit of Graz had joined with the spirit of Gothenburg and was taking off again for a new destination. It is in all of us, homeless or not, and it's up to us to feel this spirit, connect together and end poverty and homelessness in the world permanently.

16

"My life's ambition is to work with young players . . . I'd like to put something back"

Glasgow is a city of contradictions. It has a reputation for being mean and hard, while in recent times it has undergone regeneration, presenting itself as a modern, European metropolis. Like many cities throughout the world, the contradictions will always remain true – it just depends on who you happen to be.

Mark Elliot and David Duke, who have represented Scotland in the Homeless World Cup, have felt the cold end of what Glasgow can offer. They became homeless through different circumstances and it's something they would rather forget. Both have moved on in their lives, but are prepared to talk about their experiences if it can help others.

Homelessness came to Mark when he was sixteen. His parents divorced four years previously and his mother was to become involved in an abusive relationship that would culminate in her death. Mark moved in with his father and his new stepmother. By his own admission, this was a troubled house and he quickly left home and was able to find a house in Castlemilk, a large housing estate on the outskirts of the city.

"I couldn't wait to get away from my father's place but I wasn't capable of running the house in Castlemilk by myself and there were a lot of problems, so I became homeless and ended up in the hostel system."

For many years, the local authorities in Glasgow have provided shelter for homeless people through their hostel system. The hostels are large impersonal places, Dickensian in atmosphere and run in the same way as a prison. It is easy to be sucked into drug abuse, bullying and violence.

The problem has been well recorded. Glasgow City Council, backed by the Scottish Executive, have embarked on a long-term strategy to overhaul the system by decommissioning the large hostels and replacing them with smaller units run by appropriately-trained staff.

This new system, which is currently in the process of being implemented, was not in place when Mark ended up presenting himself at Glasgow's terminus for assessing homeless people, the Hamish Allen Centre. Mark was subsequently shunted off to the Bell Street Hostel.

"It was horrible. Bell Street was the worst experience of my life but it opened my eyes to homelessness. It was full of old men who were alcoholics or young guys who were full of heroin. There was nothing in between.

"I never considered myself to have any problems when I went into the system, I just didn't have a house. I was lonely, had little money, and was unable to see a way out. I became severely depressed. I was incapable of working and I was just sinking into a deeper and deeper hole.

"There are a lot of drugs in the hostels and the peer pressure is very strong. I considered drugs, just to escape from reality but I had the intelligence to realise that this was the wrong path to go down.

"I then heard about a scheme which had started where people could play football. It was called the First Steps project, run by the Queens Cross Housing Association, which was designed to encourage youth enterprise through motivational schemes. There was a Street League and I managed to join it."

Mark participated enthusiastically in a number of training sessions. He went through a series of selection processes before being given the chance to represent his country in Graz. He describes the experience as "surreal".

"You've got to remember that I was just a homeless boy from Glasgow and suddenly I was catapulted into the lime-light. I was given superstar status and was being treated as if I was a real football star with people coming up to me in the street and asking me for autographs. I felt seven-foot high.

"But it wasn't just the football. I was meeting people from other countries and beginning to realise that I wasn't alone. I also began to appreciate how much I did actually have. Maybe it wasn't much, but it was more than some of the players from Africa and I began to appreciate that. I learned a lot. The whole experience altered my life. It really did. I changed completely and realised how much I actually had inside of me. I suddenly had motivation, confidence and a reason for not lying in bed all day. And I came back from Graz and started to look at coaching football as a possible line of work."

Mark has now obtained coaching certificates at different levels, which allows him to teach children and operate with an official licence. He has been coaching the Maryhill Heart under-10 football team for over six months and also works with Queens Cross youth groups.

"My life's ambition is to work with young players and

hopefully bring the best out of them. After my experiences, I'd like to put something back."

David Duke was selected to play in the second Homeless World Cup in Gothenburg. His story is different from Mark's but his slide into homelessness is a familiar tale in Glasgow. In his early twenties, David had a good position in society with two jobs and a flat in a decent area of Glasgow. He is candid about what happened next.

"Basically, I lost my jobs because I was drinking. Without realising it, I had developed an alcohol problem and I couldn't get out of bed. I would binge for weeks and I was soon behind with the rent. The landlord subsequently kicked me out. Just like that I was homeless."

Like Mark, David arrived at the council's homeless junction point, the Hamish Allen Centre, where he was assessed and sent to the Broad Street Hostel.

"There were people recently released from prison and others totally out of it on drugs. Prostitutes and drug dealers were everywhere, and muggings happened all the time. The building was in the middle of nowhere. It was horrific. I just used to lock the door and try and sleep.

"After about a month, I found a place in the James Shields Project which was dedicated to younger people. They had an addictions project which I went to and I was able to come off the drink for periods.

"Then one day, I saw a sign on the notice board about *The Big Issue in Scotland* Challenge Cup, a competition for homeless people. I'd always played football, for my junior school, my high school and various boys clubs including Celtic Boys Club. So I went along to the competition. I knew there was a possibility of being selected to play for Scotland but to be honest I didn't think about it at the time. I just wanted to play football again.

"I'd had a drink the night before and didn't want to go but a couple of the other boys from the hostel dragged me out of bed and forced me to attend. I'll always be grateful to them because if I hadn't gone I would never have been chosen to represent my country. It was a fantastic high, better than anything you could ever get from drink.

"This really was the beginning of me distancing myself from alcohol. The addictions unit in the hostel was still supporting me but I had a new purpose – the thought of playing for Scotland was driving me on.

"At the airport, a bagpiper was there to see us off. And this was just the start. Gothenburg was simply brilliant and I had our translator tell me the Swedish word for 'friend'. I wrote it on my forehead and had a little flag of Scotland on one cheek and one of Sweden on the other. People came up to me in the street and shook my hand and kids came up and asked for my autograph.

"The experience had confirmed the change in me. I felt different."

When he returned to Glasgow, David also achieved a number of official coaching certificates. He is now involved in coaching youngsters and takes the training for the under-14 team of Mosspark Boys Club.

"There are 72 young boys involved and football keeps them off the streets and away from temptations like drink and drugs. We teach them some manners, show them how to work together as a team and respect each other."

David has been appointed as the Assistant Coach for the Scottish team in the lead-up to the 2005 event. He is naturally thrilled and is working with the manager, Jim Brown, to encourage homeless people to become involved in the football.

He has moved away from his life of alcohol, although when he talks about it, you can see it is still an issue for him. But David has won a lot of battles. His ambition is now to gain a full-time job that combines sport and community work.

"I don't have that bad a CV do I?" he says with a big grin. "After all, not many people can say they played for Scotland at football, can they? And beat Brazil into the bargain."

The successful Scottish team in Gothenburg had been managed by Jim Brown and coached by the ex-Rangers footballer, Ally Dawson. After he had finished playing professionally, Ally had stayed in the game as a coach and was involved in management for a time. He was able to offer a fascinating insight into the team, as he was able to compare and contrast the homeless squad with his past experiences with professional sides.

"It was a real issue for us and we just didn't know if it would work given the difficult circumstances the players came from. We didn't know how they were going to react, particularly given all the hype generated around their departure and the obvious excitement with the opportunities open to them.

"I'd been away with teams in my professional days and players react in different ways when you are moved to a completely different environment. So, how the players might react was the biggest concern to me and I admit to being worried about it. I could never have imagined, however, just how well they came together as a group of people.

"You always have different characters, so there were the extroverts and the ones who were quieter and it's just a question of managing that by giving them enough space to be themselves whilst building a spirit in the group. They really gelled and I think it was because we started well and began progressing through the stages.

"Some went into their shells before games while others were a bit louder, but that's okay because people deal with situations differently. The team grew in confidence and they all became stronger together. It made my job of looking after the football side of things that much easier because I was working with a group of people who were focussed.

"I didn't have to worry about them and look over my shoulder in case they were having problems settling down or were getting into trouble with other people. We were there, we were together, we mucked in with one another, just got on with it and it was absolutely fantastic."

Ally echoed the views of the coaches of Manchester United who were involved with the English side, believing the team dynamics of the event were taking the homelessness out of the players.

"You can see the change actually. We were always operating together even when we weren't playing, going on social visits like swimming in the lakes, for example. The players sometimes went off on their own, but they always said where they were going and knew they could come back at any point. The fact that there were other teams around in the same situation added to this whole dimension. Something special was going on.

"The one big similarity between this group of homeless people and the professional teams I played with is football. It unites and can bring a group of people together into a unit no matter what their background. I mean, Brazil produces the best players in the world but if you look at some of their circumstances, you see they are coming from intolerable situations yet they make it through football. The game allows you to cope with those situations very easily, I believe, and that was the big similarity between the highly-paid professional set-up and this one.

"The atmosphere during the finals was brilliant. In fact, I think the atmosphere is better than anything you'll find at a major football tournament. The audience were applauding everyone; the teams were hugging each other and the final presentation ceremony when all the teams were on the pitch together was just electric. It was amazing.

"I would admit that coaching the team and seeing their performance in Gothenburg was one of the highlights of my footballing career."

17

"If you can handle being homeless, you can put up with anything'

Homelessness in Japan affects people who are much older than those in Western Europe. During Gothenburg 2004, the Japanese squad emphasised this point by carrying around a sign marked with the number '52' – the average age of their team.

The oldest player in the tournament was Yoshinori Matsumoto. He had become homeless seven years previously, aged 58, having lost his job as a welder. As his savings dwindled, Yoshinori relied on his brothers and friends for support, but soon he found himself on the streets, living in a tent. The conditions were atrocious.

"It is as hot as sauna in the summer," he says. "And everything turns mouldy because of the humidity. There are also ticks and centipedes everywhere."

He made some money by working for street stall-keepers from time to time and by collecting aluminum cans. But it was not much. The maximum he would earn was a few hundred yen a day.

"There are homeless people who collect waste food from

garbage bins, but I've never done that. When I did not have anything, I survived by eating noodles which cost 50 yen a pack and I would eat them for days on end.

"The life of the homeless is hard emotionally. You feel very lonely and you also have to put up with the cold looks from passersby. If you can handle being homeless, you can put up with almost anything; that's how hard it is."

Yoshinori then began selling *The Big Issue Japan*, which had been established in Osaka. One day he was to hear of a football competition being organised in Sweden and Yoshinori was intrigued.

"I'd never played football before. To be honest, I did not even like sports but there were three reasons why I decided to try. Firstly, I wanted to travel abroad for the first time in my life. Secondly, because the news we hear all the time is very depressing I wanted to do something to provide me with a fun subject to talk about and thirdly, the people around me cheered and supported me a great deal when I told them about it. They helped financially and emotionally.

"One of my customers told me, 'there are not many opportunities like this that come around, so you should go'. She collected donations from her family and friends, totally 60,000 yen."

A street vendor near to Yoshinori's pitch gave him a further 1000 yen. Another customer passed him a lottery ticket and hoped that it would be the lucky stub. He was inundated with support and encouraged. And Yoshinori is very grateful for his time in Gothenburg.

"I have very good memories," he says, "especially of the warmth, goodwill and sincerity of the people. I also remember the beautiful cityscape and scenery, which made Japan feel suffocating.

"It was also interesting to communicate with representatives of the other teams. Homeless people from the various countries seemed more cheerful than those in Japan. At home, we are excluded and shunned and I wondered whether this was the same the world over. In Sweden, vendors were able to sell their papers in parks and stations with confidence. It made me think and encourage me to look forward."

Yoshinori still sells *The Big Issue Japan*. And at the age of 65 he continues to play football, turning up faithfully to the monthly practice session.

18

*"It is a little sum for one person but it makes a
big difference to the vendor"*

In 2003, they had been the only team from the African
continent. Namibia were to double that number the following
year and were to echo the spirit and friendliness that was so
apparent in the South Africa squad.

The South Africans had been brought together by *The Big
Issue Cape Town*. In Gothenburg, a twenty-five-year-old by
the name of Mziwamabhele "Bells" Hlati was to make an
impression. Pernille Berg, an intern with the Cape Town street
paper, caught up with Bells to learn more of his circumstances.

"In 2002, I finished school and went to a town called
Carletonville where my father was to look for work. I had
to start making money. But as it turned out it was very hard for
me because the workplaces required more education and skills
than I had.

"Being unemployed is a very embarrassing thing because
you are doing nothing all day. It is embarrassing because other
people see that you are not doing anything but it is worst for
yourself because you don't have a reason to wake up in the
morning.

"As a last solution I took off to Cape Town in 2003 but couldn't find anything. And then I became a vendor with *The Big Issue*. I was very eager to finally have found something to do. Selling the magazine made a great difference in my life because for the first time ever I was always ending up with some money. I came home with a little in my pocket but a lot in my heart and soul. I began to regain my self-esteem. And I was meeting more people than I had ever done.

"I especially remember one of my customers. He looked like a very important guy, with nice clothes and he was driving a Ferrari. He became a regular customer and we often had long talks together. After our first meeting I had a feeling that there was nothing I couldn't do in life – race and class didn't matter anymore.

"Some people ask a question like '*What is The Big Issue?*' I answer them by saying "it's not just a magazine, it's a lifesaver". I'll ask everyone to buy the magazine because it is a little sum for one person but it makes a big difference to the vendor.

"Football is such an amazing game. I started playing when I was thirteen years old, in the streets without a ball. We used to take off our tops and make them into something round. I was thrilled to hear about the *Big Issue* team, and I got involved immediately. And it really paid off. Travelling to the other side of the world was just so big that it was beyond anything I had ever dreamt about. It was the most amazing thing that ever happened to me.

"Being in Gothenburg was such a brilliant experience. I wanted to explore everything and made sure that I talked to people. I told them about South Africa and my culture and I listened as they talked of theirs.

"We played football in front of the school, all these different nationalities. The games would go on for the whole day and sometimes night. It was nice to be in a country where you can be outside after dark without being scared.

"When I returned to Cape Town, my fortunes began to change. One of my regular customers offered me a job as a storeman at a toy company. I had been working on my spot for almost a year and my new employer told me that I had proved to him that I was hard-working and reliable. He says he is very proud of me and hasn't regretted taking me on.

"I'm hoping to start a business course and in the future run my own business. If everything goes as planned, I will be like my current boss. I still think that anything is possible if only you work hard enough."

19

*"I changed too. I never realised the full
potential of teamwork and sport"*

Upon returning home from Gothenburg, Darryl's incredible
accomplishment was to build a house. Well, a cabin actually.
He made it from scratch with materials he found and it is
enough to hold back the Canadian winter.

Darryl has lived in the woods for years. He first started
sleeping there after he left high school when "the schizo-
phrenia took over" and he has been outside for sixteen
years. Such living is not for the faint of heart and it is
not unusual for Darryl to contend with bears and coyotes. It
also allows him to be in the company of people only when
he feels able to.

"There are times when I just don't want to be around
others," he tells Paul, who was the manager of the Canada
squad that came to Gothenburg.

"Basically when the voices are too much," explains Paul,
"Darryl has a large informal network of people who are
interested in his life and as a result provide a level of care.
When I look back I think, wow, how did we get Darryl over to
Sweden? I mean, he has a lot of mental health issues but he was

able to adapt and become part of the community. And we, in turn, were able to reach out to him and adapt ourselves.

Paul has been working with federal offenders for fifteen years and homeless people for the past eight. When he first read about the World Cup in an article in the *Washington Post*, Paul sent an e-mail to Bernhard saying he'd love to organise a Canadian team. He knew a little about football, having watched Aston Villa in England as a youngster when his father completed a two-year stint in a teacher exchange programme. Paul had also helped to establish some soccer leagues in a poor neighbourhood in Mississauga which involved over sixty youngsters. He, therefore, knew the potential of soccer.

"I'd forgotten about my request to Bernhard and then a few months later I received a response saying 'you're in'.

"My aim on leaving Canada was simply to bring everybody back. Seriously, I didn't know what to expect and I thought it would be a challenge, so just to get everyone home was a big enough goal.

"And the results didn't matter. We just had so many positive growths amongst the players. I mean the goalkeeper, Roger, changed from shouting at everybody to become much more encouraging. Another of the players, Dave, wanted to party all the time, but he came around and started to respect his colleagues. When we got back to Canada, his project worker called me to say that they had witnessed the biggest positive change in him in four years.

"This is because the Homeless World Cup takes people out of their environment and mixes them with others who are different, even if they live in similar circumstances. We are lifting them out of their box and introducing a whole new set of horizons. Then, they are involved with teams in a competitive setting which pulls them together and draws the best out of them.

"When you're at home and you're trying to do outreach to create connections with individuals, it is just so incredibly hard. What you have in the World Cup is the power of the group with everybody providing something to create collective and individual growth. I mean I changed too. I never realised the full potential of team-work and sport.

"The big problem we've got these days is that everyone is dissected and put in a silo. So you have the mental health silo and the addiction silo and so on. Then we invent terminology which acts as a barrier. Even the homeless people start using the language and labelling themselves and saying things like: 'I can't do this because I'm in the addiction silo and I can't do that because I'm in the illiterate silo.' We've created a system where everyone believes in their own label and they won't move on as a result.

"The reality is completely different. We all have different parts – not everything is black and white. The football in Gothenburg proved this – a group of people who weren't dissected or classified! It was so liberating.

Paul has helped establish some soccer games on a regular basis involving players from five different shelters. It is early days but he hopes a street league might emerge. From there it could spread across the country. At the very least, we'll be seeing him again.

"Too right," he laughs. "There'll be a Canadian team at the 2005 event."

20

"Sport is addictive. If you can awake this in
you then you have some potential solutions"

Maria Salivonenko's is not a new story. It is a familiarly
depressing tale.

"Unemployment has grown considerably – it's twenty per-
cent in some areas," she explains. "And if you add in alcohol
and drug abuse, which are also increasing, then you can see
that we have a developing problem.

Monar was set up in 1978. It now has thirty drug centres
and around sixty centres for homeless people throughout
Poland. The organisation has always believed that sport can
be play a central part in rehabilitation. And since its inception,
Monar have arranged annual winter and summer camps that
involve such activities as football and mountaineering. Their
success comes as no surprise to Maria. She has long been
convinced about the role of sport.

"It is very optimistic and in some ways, sport is addictive," she
says. "If you can awake this in you then you have some potential
solutions. It encourages people to discover themselves and to
explore inside their inner self. It is very emotional."

Maria believes it goes beyond social assistance and traditional social work. She thinks that these disciplines have their justified role in society but she contends that if people are to change then they must do something for themselves.

"Sitting around waiting for help and remaining passive won't solve anything. In a very instinctive manner, sport is a natural way to make a person become active and wake up to the possibilities open to them. How good or bad you are is irrelevant. You are woken from your passive state and realise what you can do for yourself."

In early 2004, Monar coordinated the different shelters and projects throughout the country into street soccer competitions. This would lead to a national championship where the final squad would be selected. Poland were to finish third in the 2004 Homeless World Cup and have since developed into one of the top street soccer nations. Marek Sosczak is their goalkeeper.

"I lived with my grandmother in a flat which belonged to the city," he tells Maria. "The family neglected to arrange ownership and, as a result, after the death of my grandmother, I had no right to occupy the apartment any more. I was forced to leave.

"After the death of my grandmother, I started to rent rooms whenever I was able to pay for it. But soon I couldn't afford it and I could no longer intrude on my friends' lives and on their hospitality. I ended up in a shelter for homeless people.

"I felt horrible, hopeless and like I was in another world. It is not that the people there were unkind or that the rooms were dirty. It was just different people, a different life and many rules. Later on I got used to people in the shelter and made friends with them, eventually convincing several guys to start playing soccer.

"In spring 2004, our shelter soccer team was invited by Monar and Artur Hyżyk, their coach, to take part in the selection process for the Homeless World Cup. And I was fortunate.

"The actual matches in Gothenburg were very exciting! I ask myself why we won so many games over there – I think it is because, when you play, you feel like you are flying. All that adrenaline just takes you forward.

"The spectators were fun and were very kind and friendly. Apart from watching games they would also come to the players' village to talk to us. And I think that, yes, I have changed for the better. I started to feel people's respect towards me, and began feeling more secure.

"I work as a carpenter now and see my fourteen-year-old daughter every weekend. I might still live in a shelter but I am working hard towards getting an apartment. This is my dream and I have a plan. But I cannot tell you about that. I am afraid to do so would bring me bad luck."

21

*"All those homeless people playing with such
emotion, it's really hard to describe without
doing it justice or seeming to exaggerate"*

Peter Muller loves the Homeless World Cup. He bumped into it
quite by chance when visiting Graz with his family during the
summer of 2003. Wandering through the city's streets, he heard
a series of noises coming from nearby. At first, he thought it was
outdoor theatre. But the closer he got, the more Peter saw that it
was an altogether different kind of drama.

"It was an unforgettable experience. There was something
magic about it. All those young homeless people playing
football for their country with such emotion, it's really hard
to describe without failing to do it justice or seeming to
exaggerate.

"For me, it was the combination of the speed of the games
allied with the spirit in which the whole thing was played
which made it so attractive. Some of the players had real skill
and what they could do with the ball in such a small space was
incredible. There were obviously people who were not so good
but they were enjoying themselves so much that it simply
rubbed off on everyone who was watching."

Peter has followed developments via the web site. He doesn't watch much professional football but his ears prick up at the mention of street soccer.

"I just think it's so much more of a real game. These big stadiums with their overpaid actors are just becoming something different. I followed what was going on in Gothenburg. I wished I'd been there. But I have one great memory and that's enough."

Rosie Kane MSP, who sits in the Scottish Parliament representing the Scottish Socialist Party, was to help raise money for the Scottish squad that journeyed to Gothenburg.

"I normally don't like football or what it stands for," she said. "But this is different. Our team is the pride of Scotland. They will come onto the field with the 'Flower of Scotland' playing, but they are more used to sleeping among the flowers."

It was in the Swedish city that Rosie was to become totally hooked on street soccer. She was not there in any official capacity, but simply as a fan. Writing in her regular column in the *Sunday Mail* newspaper at the time, she summed up the mood wonderfully.

"That's it, folks, I'm converted. I have seen the light and I am now a footy fan – official. I have screamed like a complete bam from the sidelines and called the ref names that would shock a sailor. I have draped myself from head to toe in the Saltire and have proudly sung 'Flower of Scotland' in the streets of Gothenburg until I'm hoarse. All thanks to our magnificent Homeless World Cup squad."

Rosie is also aware and appreciative of the international flavour of the event and the connections that were made between the various nations.

"These guys not only share their love of the beautiful game, they also share the knowledge of homelessness. It is this awareness that is the glue that holds the teams together away from the pitch."

Speaking after her return home she told me that this had probably been her best holiday ever. Rosie has been converted. Not to the game that is shown on television every other day, however, but to a street game which featured participants a world away from the likes of today's soccer superstars.

Indeed, Rosie had only planned to come along to watch the first four days of the tournament because she had to be in Scotland for the marriage of a good friend. But as the competition drew her in and the atmosphere began to build, Rosie called to say she'd have to miss the wedding and she altered her plane tickets accordingly.

While the watching public was giving a collective thumbs-up, the media were also becoming engrossed. As they filed their stories, I would canvass opinions. Tim Walker, the director of the Real Sports HBO documentary was fulsome in his praise.

"It is quite simply awesome and something I never would have believed possible," he told me. "I've got to do a thirty-minute documentary but I could make a programme which could go on for hours. It's going to be really hard to edit."

So what is it that makes the Homeless World Cup so compelling? Why do people find it "awesome"? Doesn't the same atmosphere exist at every major sporting event, especially where teams from all over the world are involved? What's so different? Journalists are normally a cynical bunch but in Graz and Gothenburg they weren't behaving as clichés.

Perhaps the answer is best summed up by one of the cameramen at Graz who was working for the global news agency, Reuters.

"Nowadays," he began, "the journalists are corralled at the bigger sporting events, particularly football. You aren't given real access. It's controlled and stage-managed with agents here and officials there and you are simply pushed into showing what they want you to show. They have a formula, which they think obviously works, but it's all becoming a bit synthetic and plastic. You only see the players at pre-arranged press conferences and that's that.

"Whereas here you have access all the time and everything is run in a very relaxed way. The media are welcomed and almost become part of the show. It's a bit rough and ready, right enough, but so what, this is what sport should be all about: open, enjoyable, entertaining and friendly. And you've got the lot here."

I tried to find critics. Honestly.

"I wish the German team were better," joked one German reporter when asked about what could be improved. That we were unable to do. But with an enthralled audience of spectators and media, our task was to ensure the Homeless World Cup kept on progressing.

Crucially, we have to keep the close connection between the fans and the event. While we strive for efficiency in the running of the tournament, we cannot allow anyone to become excluded in the process. The Homeless World Cup will always be about inclusion.

22

". . . not only did we help change the image of homeless people, but we helped change the image of asylum seekers as well"

The performance of the Austrian team surprised many. And delighted even more. There were great celebrations and the squad appeared on television, were introduced to politicians and given ovations by an admiring public. They were the World Champions after all. But the squad were also all asylum seekers: Angus Okanume was one of those players.

Born in 1985 in the Nigerian city of Onisha, Angus was seventeen when he entered Austria illegally. He had to flee his native country due to rising religious tension between Christians and the Muslim Sharia movements. As the former, Angus felt his life was in danger and he paid those involved in people-trafficking to help him leave the country.

Once in Graz, he was taken care of by Caritas, the charity backed by the Catholic Church. Angus lives in an asylum shelter and despite being in the country for over two years, his case is still to be examined by the authorities. This is not unusual in a country where such cases can take up to ten years.

Angus was to receive a boost following his performance in

Graz. The media exposure opened many doors and he has been able to participate in sporting activities, enroll in an education programme and integrate into Austrian society. He feels warmly towards his adopted country and is comfortable in his surroundings. This was not always the case. In the beginning, life proved difficult for Angus.

"I had to deal with many new things. First, the food was not easy to get used to for an African. And it was also hard to realise that some people have negative attitudes towards black people. They do not see you as a person but only that you are black. Or they might suspect that you are dealing with drugs, which is a very common prejudice against asylum seekers.

"And oh yes. I'd never seen snow in my life before and there's a lot in Austria. That's probably the funniest experience I've had. The best moments, however, were making friends at the Homeless World Cup. It was just so great to play football, to have African friends and to play in front of an appreciative audience. And, of course, to win the Cup for Austria was a real thrill."

Angus had made the team following qualifications which involved a competition between teams from all the major cities in Austria. Graz won the qualifying stage and Angus was selected to play for the national side.

"The really great moments were meeting other players from different nations. It showed me the many situations people come from and what homelessness looks like around the world."

The Austrian people were naturally proud of their players. This was indeed a fine success, which had been played in front of a global audience. But after the party, there is always a new dawn.

"It was hard for us, the World Champions, to return to our lives as asylum seekers. The Homeless World Cup had given me great motivation and I really wanted to move on in my life. As an asylum seeker, however, you have to be patient and wait for your status to alter. But I have found confidence now and am sure opportunities will begin to open up."

For Harald Schmied, one of the instigators and organisers of the tournament, there was natural delight in the host nation winning. But he was philosophical, observing that people were celebrating an Austrian victory that had come with a team made up entirely of players that were born outside of Austria.

"I think this is very important for the work we are doing," he said. "Because it not only proves that homeless people can perform to the highest level, but it shows what a contribution asylum seekers can make to Austria and this is something that is sometimes lost on people. Hopefully, in terms of perception, not only did we help change the image of homeless people, but we helped change the image of asylum seekers as well. Perhaps this is a double triumph in Austria."

23

"I was a pariah and I reminded them of what they might become"

No international football competition is complete unless Brazil is involved. Not only do they provide magic on the field, they also supply sunshine off it, with their samba bands and their dancing rhythms. The Homeless World Cup was no different.

In January 2005, staff and vendors from the street paper *OCAS*, which is sold in São Paulo, made their way to Porto Alegre. They were there to participate in the World Social Forum, a large annual event involving civil society groups from around the world.

Three of the players who represented Brazil in the Homeless World Cup in Gothenburg talked to Luciano Rocco, the editor of *OCAS*. Their individual experiences are different, yet there is a unifying bond. Being homeless on the streets of São Paolo is very hard and its grim reality brings them together. They each talk of discrimination, humiliation and of being invisible.

Antônio Cesar Andrade da Silva is 30 now but first became homeless at the age of six. He was picked up by the authorities and remained in a child welfare reformatory, before ending up back on the streets.

Irany Francisco dos Reis is 41 and admits to becoming homeless because he drank too much *cachaça*, a Brazilian alcoholic drink made of sugar cane. Cláudio Bongiovani is 52 and ended up on the streets after his family was killed in a car crash.

"I went out of my mind," he says. "I was like a crazy man, lost, and without direction. The worst moment was when I was unable to see my children and my wife as the coffins had already been sealed. Apparently, they were too badly burned.

"I guess this memory has brought the biggest weight to my heart. It tortured me. But with the help of *OCAS*, I found new strength from inside. I began to have human relationships, living with groups of people and doing things with them. In the streets you lose everything but this gave me my manhood back. I found my self-esteem and my character rose. Without *OCAS*, I cannot bear to think what might have been."

It was in 1999 that Irany reached his lowest point. His life was dominated by alcohol.

"I was on the streets, talking with myself," he says. "It was no surprise that I was to end up in a psychiatric clinic."

"The streets are not glamorous," interjects Antônio. "They are not safe for anyone," and he remembers the days of hunger, rain and abject misery. But Antônio describes people as generally being warm to him, and he was never hit or threatened. Irany and Cláudio do not offer similar sentiments.

"You feel discrimination on the streets," states Irany. "I searched for food and I never opened my hand for charity. If I had some money I might go into a snack bar but as soon as I walked in I could feel their discrimination. I felt bad enough in myself. I was a pariah and I reminded them of what they might become.

"People just didn't want to know, if alcohol has been involved. They consider you a loser and a fool. But in reality, there are many homeless people more competent than those who live in houses.'

When OCAS announced that they were organising a team to represent Brazil at the Homeless World Cup, all three were interested.

"We had training on Tuesdays and Thursdays," recalls Cláudio. "Nobody knew much about soccer. The trainer ended the sessions with his head full. He used to say one thing and we'd do another thing. There were quarrels but slowly he managed to create a group and we became increasingly united."

"We trained below a viaduct in Brás, a neighbourhood on the east side of São Paulo," remembers Irany. "I didn't even have the appropriate shoes and the ball was really old."

But the training sessions slowly came together and the squad departed for Gothenburg.

"It doesn't compare to anything in my life," says Cláudio. "First, just being in a foreign country and then because of the treatment we received when we were there. We were so well treated. When we walked along the streets people cried, 'Brazil, Brazil'."

"In soccer terms, the tournament was disappointing," maintains Irany. "I'm not a hypocrite and it's bad to lose, let's be honest. Mainly when we come from the streets we want to win. And I want to win in life.

"In my opinion, teams from the other countries are more prepared to face the world, psychologically speaking. Brazilians have an exaggerated selfishness. We are more concerned with taking advantage of situations and we haven't learnt to share.

"In Gothenburg, I saw men taking a bath together and I saw more solidarity between them. In Brazil, adult homeless people don't see a union. I have lived on the streets for 10 years. Homeless street children are more united. One stands for the other, even if they have problems amongst themselves."

"We had the opportunity to meet people from more developed countries," relates Cláudio. "And they have a better ground to stand on than us. But we found out about the other street papers and we were able to compare them with ours. We were able to bring some ideas back to Brazil."

The three men continue to talk, focussing on the changes they have made in their own lives as a result of their involvement in the competition.

"I changed a lot, not much possibly in social and financial terms because I am still a vendor with *OCAS*," explains Cláudio. "But now we speak about the project with great enthusiasm and are more conscious of what we are doing. We united our strengths, and nowadays share responsibilities. Through this experience we are turning into better people – people who are raising themselves."

"My self-esteem has been rebuilt," says Irany. "When I came back from Gothenburg I kept living in the hostel selling *OCAS* and my sales increased. I am in touch with people who believe in other human beings. The public like the magazine and encourage me a lot.

"I'm studying now. I'm starting secondary school this year and intend to take a preparatory course to try to enter university. I'd like to take a course which has an association with *OCAS*. My aim is to study literature at the Universidade de São Paulo. Even if I don't succeed, it will be a great experience. But I believe I can succeed because I'm really dedicated to my studies."

Antônio is also studying and the three friends plan to take part in future Homeless World Cups.

"I've just started to train again," Cláudio says, "and I

believe our preparation will be much better this time. In 2004, I wasn't prepared. In my mind, I had to win in all areas. It's difficult to explain but it's not only the physical which matters, it's the psychological side as well. This time I'll be ready."

24

"It was embarrassing. But better than dropping the ball, I suppose"

Twenty-two-year-old Kevin Wilson won the Best Goalkeeper Award in Gothenburg. It was unfortunate that he dropped the trophy just after it had been handed to him.

"It was embarrassing," he recalls. "But better than dropping the ball, I suppose."

Kevin became homeless when he was just seventeen. He had been living with foster parents from a very young age and had to leave because he had reached an age when he was no longer categorised as a child.

"I didn't have anywhere to go and I ended up on the streets. It was not for long, however, just a few nights. The local council found me a house but there was a lot of trouble and it was totally unsuitable for me. So, I ended up at SHAP."

The Single Homeless Accommodation Project (SHAP) is based in Huddersfield and Kevin has been attached to it since he first had to leave his foster home. He has been playing for their football team for the past three years.

"We've done quite well actually, winning a couple of tournaments and coming second in some others. We set up a league at Huddersfield Sports Centre and play against other projects like us."

Kevin heard that trials were being organised for a team to represent England at the Homeless World Cup in Gothenburg. The trials were open to homeless people who had played some football, so Kevin went along to Manchester United's Cliff training ground to see if he could win a place in the squad.

"The training facilities were brilliant but nothing like the facilities at Carrington, Manchester's other training ground, where we trained later on; they were totally amazing.

"The first couple of trials involved playing matches so the coaches could see what level you were at and the second part involved fitness exercises, as well as getting to know your team mates.

"There must have been over a thousand people there from all over the place and gradually the numbers were whittled down. The final names were read out and I was on the plane to Gothenburg and, well, I was over the moon. I had been selected to play for England and it was to be one of the greatest experiences of my life. After all, there's not many people who get to play football for their country."

Kevin's foster parents were to arrive in Gothenburg. It was a surprise visit and, while he was thrilled, England's goalkeeper became a little nervous and in an effort to impress made a couple of mistakes.

"I was really taken aback to see them sitting in the front row and I think I let in about five goals and we were easily beaten. But we qualified from that section anyway, so it was okay," he smiles.

Gothenburg will always hold fond memories for Kevin. It wasn't just the football, the arrival of his foster parents, the grand architecture of the Scandinavian city and the admiring crowds.

"It was just a tremendous experience. I mean, we met lots of other really good people. We got on really well with the Scottish team and the Irish and I made a lot of new friends. It was brilliant just meeting people from other countries, mixing with them and getting to know them.

"The crowds were amazing. I think 40,000 people came to watch during the week and there were 2,000 at some games. I've never played in fronts of crowds that size before and it is something you just never imagine will happen."

Back in England, Kevin kept playing football and played for England again in a special event involving the four home nations – England, Scotland, Ireland and Wales. The competition was played at Manchester United's training ground and Wales won the inaugural trophy in an event which will now take place every year.

"It was great to meet up again with some of the people who had been in Gothenburg. Wales weren't expected to win but they deserved it in the end. A couple of the Manchester United players, Wes Brown and Alan Smith, were there and they talked to us for a while. It's good to be taken seriously."

Kevin remains with the SHAP project but his future prospects look very bright. Because he is still with SHAP, he is still eligible to take part in trials for the English team for 2005. Kevin remains hopeful of selection.

"Well, we all have to start over again," he explains. "We just don't get re-selected. Once again, there are hundreds of people trying to get on the team, so it certainly isn't straightforward."

Away from the pressures of the selection process, Kevin has nearly finished his Level One FA Coaching Course. He is hopeful of a sports-related job, with football being his preferred option. The course is organised through a "football in the community" scheme run under the auspices of the local professional club, Huddersfield Town.

"Once I complete the course, I will be able to coach kids between the ages of four and sixteen," he tells me proudly. And no doubt pass on his memories of the Homeless World Cup.

25

*"Wouldn't half the players be denied entry and
sent home?"*

The amount of planning that was becoming necessary to host
the Homeless World Cup meant that the venues required as
much time as possible in order to piece together the compo-
nents properly. During the 2004 annual INSP conference in
Glasgow, therefore, we were to announce the successful bids
for the 2005 and 2006 tournaments.

The Big News (New York) and *The Big Issue Cape Town*
had presented well-thought-out plans that were exciting and
feasible. Thus, the 2005 and 2006 events were handed to the
respective cities.

I was particularly pleased that these bids had been
successful. On a sentimental level, Cape Town was the
city where the idea was first mooted. But the decision was
not based upon sentiment. South Africa was rife with
homelessness and we were also aware of the love of sports
the nation had. I was already imagining an outstanding
spectacle and was additionally thrilled by the thought of
bringing the Homeless World Cup to the southern hemisphere.

New York would also provide a stunning, if different back-drop, to the tournament. The city seemed a natural place for street soccer to be played. And with the announcement coming three months ahead of the Gothenburg event, New York would have over a year to plan.

Jeff Grunberg, chief executive of the Grand Central Neigh-bourhood Social Service Co-operation, which runs *Big News*, was to co-ordinate the 2005 tournament from the American end. He immediately set up a committee involving key people from the world of business, media and public services. His brother, Ron, was involved from the street paper side, while Cecelia Hoffman was appointed from within Jeff's organisa-tion to run matters on a daily basis.

Bryant Park was selected as the venue. This well-managed city park, a green oasis in Midtown Manhattan between Fifth and Sixth Avenue and next to the Public Library, was sur-rounded on four sides by colossal skyscrapers. It would capture the traditional image of New York and provide a magnificent setting for players and spectators alike.

The history of the park seemed to make it an even more appropriate choice. It was renamed in 1884 in the honour of William Cullen Bryant, who had been a civic reformer, news-paper editor and poet. In more recent times, the area had fallen into disrepute, becoming a haunt for muggers and drug deal-ers. But Bryant Park was to be transformed, soon to become a spot for relaxing and eating in the surrounding cafes, or viewing the many concerts and displays that are put on. It had changed out of all recognition and was an embodiment of what the Homeless World Cup was trying to do: reform and transform.

The Sports Commission for the Mayor's Office was in-volved and very keen to aid the event. HBO were to be our media partners, and Ross Greenburg, President of HBO

Sports, was to prove an enthusiastic supporter. Having him on board really helped to add weight to Jeff's co-ordinating committee.

Ron, along with Jeff and Cecelia, arrived in Gothenburg to view the event at close quarters. There was plenty to observe. There were eight more teams, the crowd numbers had doubled, the number of media enquiries had grown considerably and expectations were very high all round. In retrospect, we had underestimated the amount of work needed to go into this bigger event and the well-oiled organisation that had been in Graz was showing signs of strain. It was obvious that we would have to alter the structure in the future, particularly as we wanted the tournament to grow. The sheer scale of the event, combined with our own ambitious objectives, would mean that our operating method had to be improved. Most of the street papers were small and to foist a major international event onto their already overloaded resources was impractical.

A decision was made to hire an event management company with experience in sports. It made sense, given the resources we had at our disposal, and it was felt that the event company could make a significant difference in attracting sponsorship. We didn't want to fall into the trap of growing too fast too quickly, but we wanted to build on the obvious success of Graz and Gothenburg.

Bryant Park initially looked problematic due to its availability in the summer months, the strict rules governing what could and could not be done in the park, and the cost of hiring the space. But these issues could be resolved given a little time and discussion. And I've always been an admirer of the American "can do" attitude. Everyone seemed determined to make New York 2005 something to remember.

It was during a meeting in Gothenburg that someone first broached the issue of entry into the US.

"Wouldn't half the players be denied entry and sent home?" they asked.

I replied that part of the deal for accepting the bid from New York was assurances that all matters relating to entry would be determined well in advance. We couldn't have a situation whereby teams were excluded from participating in their own tournament. As a cautionary measure, a deadline had been set. If we were unable to receive the necessary guarantees from the authorities, then we would look for an alternative venue in Europe.

Harald, Bernhard and I visited New York in October 2004, to sort out contractual issues, monitor progress and make sure that all was running smoothly. There were the usual organisational issues, associated with putting on any event, but all seemed to be on course – with the exception of the players' entry visas.

Our lawyers, White and Case, which had offices in New York, had been very helpful in explaining the exact situation in terms of the law. They had also introduced us to the relevant people at the Department of Homeland Security. Bernhard travelled down to Washington to meet with the officials and the atmosphere was positive. The prevailing attitude seemed to be that a solution was more than likely.

We had always been honest about the circumstances surrounding our players. Some may have criminal records, and others will have a history of substance and alcohol abuse. But the point of our scheme was that this was now behind them. The Americans understood. As we left the US, we believed there to be challenges ahead but nothing that would prove insurmountable.

Unfortunately, this was not to be the case. Our deadline was approaching and still there was no definite conclusion to the matter of entry visas. We extended the date, as our lawyers continued in discussion with Homeland Security, but still no guarantees were forthcoming. We were left to make a desperate decision. New York 2005 was to be cancelled.

Jeff and his colleagues were extremely upset. The best the US authorities were offering was that we could fly teams into the country, have lawyers on standby at the airports and deal with the issues as they arose. We could not take such a risk.

I was downhearted and depressed. Although there was enthusiasm and support from a number of influential American sources, we were unable to get beyond bureaucracy. This was our greatest disappointment and our heads went down. But we resolved that we were not going to be beaten. We had to come up with an alternative.

26

*"It is also an ideal opportunity to raise
awareness and challenge perceptions about
what homeless people can achieve"*

The New York decision had been deflating. With the exception of the Cameroon situation in Gothenburg, we had been on a roll. This, we determined, would not be an ending.

Word had got out regarding the 2005 cancellation and a number of cities stepped in, offering to host the tournament. Bernhard, Harald and I thought about it long and hard. We were in an emergency situation, and practical solutions were required. It was then I suggested Edinburgh and that I would take control of the organisation.

Apart from being an incredibly attractive city, Edinburgh was readily accessible and was used to hosting major international events all year round. This was the good news. The downside was that we only had six months in which to pull everything together.

I began making telephone calls. The key seemed to be gaining the support from the City of Edinburgh Council and I quickly made an appointment to see Steve Cardownie, the Deputy Convenor.

He brought along Councillor Ricky Henderson, the executive member for Sports, Culture and Leisure, and the response was immediately positive. Edinburgh was suddenly looking like a possibility and further discussions were to bring the event close to reality.

A key senior Scottish Government official, Malcolm Chisholm, the Communities Minister, agreed to meet. With Nike having already committed to help, and the City of Edinburgh Council agreeable, I felt that if the Scottish Executive was to come on board, then I would be confident enough to say that we could proceed with Edinburgh as the 2005 venue.

The Minister welcomed me and seemed genuinely interested in what I was to say. He had been well briefed and our discussion revolved around the benefits the tournament would bring to Scotland and to homeless people. By the close of the meeting, he had offered his support and asked that I work with his department on drawing up a plan, which would include some financial support.

Strong foundations were being laid. There was still an element of risk and a mass of work ahead. But we had created a momentum. The Scottish Football Association provided their blessing and the decision was taken. The capital of Scotland would host the 2005 Homeless World Cup, starting on July 19th.

The official announcement was made in mid-February and the Scottish Executive pledged £30,000 and brought in additional financial support through its agencies, Event Scotland and Sport Scotland.

Speaking at the launch, Malcolm Chisholm said he was delighted to confirm the Scottish Executive's support for the Homeless World Cup.

"The social impact of an event such as this is clear and the Homeless World Cup has a strong positive impact on participants," he said. "It is also an ideal opportunity to raise awareness and challenge perceptions about what homeless people can achieve."

Councillor Ricky Henderson, Executive Member for Sport, Culture and Leisure for the City of Edinburgh Council, was to add, "Edinburgh has a great reputation for hosting international events and the 2005 Homeless World Cup is coming to Scotland's capital knowing they can expect a warm welcome. We're looking forward to a memorable and successful tournament for everyone who comes to participate and spectate."

There was a lot to do. And there still is, at the time of writing. But we were determined to repay the city of Edinburgh for its kind backing. And we are thrilled that the journey of the Homeless World Cup keeps on going.

27

"If there are people who care about the homeless, I myself must be responsible for my life. I must be the first to take care of me"

The world these days demands information. Everything must be analysed, dissected and categorised. We live in an age of information overload. Sometimes, it feels like the public reference library has invaded our brains. "I can take no more," I hear myself saying sometimes.

Used correctly, of course, information is liberating. The more information we have at our fingertips, the more likely it is we can argue and win our point. The increased availability of the web and its growth allows us much greater access. It has to be positive. But, too often, I find that excessive information is obscuring the conclusion.

There are people who pride themselves in giving elaborate power-point presentations containing, well, lots of . . . information. It is such a turnoff. No-one can possibly take in what is being displayed. It becomes boring and irrelevant and the main message of the presentation is totally lost. A good presenter will only use a power-point as back up to emphasise key points. Too often these days, the power-point takes over.

I've always been a bit anti when it comes to research and analysis concerning homelessness. The public sector, in particular, wants to justify its spending and to establish if its strategy is working. There is plenty of logic in all this but it is just overdone. There's too much of it and it's overanalysed to such a point that it becomes irrelevant.

If we are working with someone who has a drug problem but is making steady progress in dealing with the problem, how exactly do you measure it? Leaving homelessness is never a linear progression. You have good days and bad days, you go forwards and backwards. All I can say is that this person is making overall progress, so that has to be good. Anecdotal evidence can be so much more powerful and, indeed, relevant.

We are all human beings. Homeless people and those living in poverty are human beings. They are not items which can be measured. Sure, we can observe and learn and make recommendations which hopefully lead to solutions. To me, the overall objective is to end homelessness altogether. We do that by working together and by creating inclusive societies where we respect each other.

Having said this, we can't operate in a bubble and just ignore the way of the world. We have to work with current practices while making our point. One of the standard questions journalists ask us all the time is: what happens to the players after the tournament? Other people, particularly those working with homeless and excluded people, ask the same question as well. It's perfectly valid and we are able to answer and illustrate our conviction that sports can destroy marginalisation by giving many individual examples of players who are no longer homeless.

But, for our overall objectives, this is not enough. We have to do more. So, we have organised an impact report following the Gothenburg tournament.

I remember being challenged by a speech former President Bill Clinton made at the beginning of 2004. He was talking about the onset of globalisation and relating this to the problems in the world. He talked about solutions and said that it was just not acceptable to have a small local project somewhere in the world which was, let's say, very successful in tackling poverty. There was, he maintained, a moral imperative to take that project to scale in order that it could make a major impact in the world. He challenged both the global institutions to gear up in order to create systems and capital to deal with demand and he challenged those who were running small projects to look at the world rather than just what was in front of them.

I was challenged. I thought he was right on one level. I could see what he meant about globalisation. If the big companies have used all sorts of unregulated channels to make huge amounts of money through globalisation, then why shouldn't other organisations which had a completely different set of values, use the same methods to get what they wanted? What he was saying was very practical and it appealed to me.

On the other hand, the whole notion of scale bothered me. In my experience, many of the problems in the world seemed to be related to "bigness". Why would we want to create a large global institution with all its associated and costly bureaucracy? Institutions also bring with them unnecessary governance and all the associated political issues. So much time is spent on running the institution rather than concentrating on the job at hand. Why would we want to scale Mount Everest when we could easily conquer many more foothills? His challenge was too hard and not one that would be effective anyway.

But I couldn't get Clinton's words out of my head. By this point, I'd seen just how successful the Graz event had been and

Gothenburg was coming up as well. In a tiny, tiny way we had demonstrated that we had found something which gave answers. There is so much poverty in the world that if we find a solution, then we need to tell everyone immediately. We need to scream it from the rooftops. We would hope someone else could hear us and pick up the baton and apply what we had found to their own situation. Perhaps, Clinton had a point.

After all, this was how the street papers had spread throughout the world. It had happened organically after people in different countries saw how something which was very practical could be applied to their own country. But it had happened in a haphazard way. It could have been so much more effective. If this street football with homeless people could be taken to scale in an organised way then we could make a major impact globally.

The answer was staring us in the face. We needed to build a very small global infrastructure which allowed individual projects in cities and countries in the world to grow and expand. So, we would concentrate on marketing the Homeless World Cup but it would only be the tip of the iceberg because, underneath the surface, individual projects would be operating in different cities around the world, all connected together through the Homeless World Cup. We would expand and encourage country championships, continental cups and so on to start. We could maybe have the European championships, for example, and we would encourage countries to play each other. It's already happening.

But first, we had to prove that street soccer did indeed provide solutions. We had to keep the people who need absolute proof and want detailed information informed about the wisdom of what we do. We had carried out some research after the Graz tournament but we decided to carry out a more comprehensive survey after the Gothenburg event.

The results are staggering. Even by our own claims, I was amazed at the significant impact the Homeless World Cup had made on people's lives. Boldly, then, here are some facts and figures.

The number of national teams taking part increased from 18 to 26 national teams which in turn meant that the number of players involved increased from 141 to 204. The application process for the upcoming 2005 Homeless World Cup in Scotland indicates a further growth with up to 32 participating nations.

More than 90% of the players reported a major change in their lifestyles. This is a very significant percentage in any language.

The players report that they have a generally higher self esteem and also have a much better motivation for life. Participants have found employment and improved their own housing situation. They report much better social relations including several family reunions which took place after the World Cup. Those who remained with the street papers have much stronger engagement with the publication. All of them have developed a much better attitude towards health. A very high percentage of the players (72%) continued playing football together after the World Cup compared with only 36% who played on a regular basis before.

Seventy-eight players (38%) moved on from being a street paper vendor or being unemployed to have regular jobs. The jobs varied from a miner to a shop assistant, right through to setting up their own businesses or becoming football coaches. Some players actually started working as organisers in their own street paper project. Maxim Mastitski from Russia, for example, studies social management to support the St. Petersburg street paper project, *Put Domoi*. The Swedish team captain, Tajmaz David Nilsson, became managing coach of the Swedish national team for the Homeless World Cup 2005.

Sixteen of the 204 players who took part in Gothenburg now make their living partly from football by signing with professional and semi-professional teams in their countries, as either coaches or as players. England, Ireland, Ukraine, Sweden, Scotland and Russia all have examples. Ahmet Akdag, one of the English players, signed at Bromley Football Club in England while the outstanding goalkeeper in Gothenburg, Kevin Wilson, also from England, has finished his coaching course and was nominated for Sports Personality of the Year in the Yorkshire Area. The top goal scorer in Gothenburg, Yevgen Adamenko, plays for a professional club in his native Ukraine. These players are now not only involved in regular training and competitions but also have a stabilised lifestyle including good housing and regular income.

Players' lives have changed, many significantly. However, changing the player's life situation has a different meaning in each of the participating countries. Improving the life status of a homeless person looks quite different in Switzerland compared to Namibia or Ukraine. In wealthy industrialised nations, the emphasis tends to lie more with integration than education. Drug treatments linked to employment and housing are seen as essential. Education or training is seen as vital for asylum seekers, for example. An improvement in housing as a catch-all solution is not seen as the main issue. An apparently acceptable housing situation including social housing or living with the family is not always the whole solution.

In the southern hemisphere the situation is very different. For a player in Namibia or South Africa, for example, finding a job or managing to get into some form of education will mean a significant improvement in their living situation. Even if the player's immediate housing situation may change, or indeed deteriorate, his status is altered. In Ukraine, as in other countries, alcohol and drug abuse have proved to be a significant problem. Moving on in these situations, means tackling these problems and entry into education can make a much greater impact than finding a roof over your head.

The key aspect from the impact report shows that the vast majority of players are making major inroads into changing their lives which will, in the end, mean that they are no longer homeless. Some will choose education or employment or even playing football as a start point before thinking about their housing. The process has started and even more significant changes will occur.

The overall impact figures show that 74% (151 players) have significantly changed their living situation after the Homeless World Cup 2004 by either finding jobs, improving their housing situation, choosing an education or by undergoing drug treatment.

- 38% (78 players) have a regular job
- 46% (95 players) improved their housing situation
- 34% (70 players) chose education including back-to-work courses, further education and schooling
- 27% (56 players) have had a drug dependency issue addressed

All the street papers which formed teams for the World Cup report a higher profile for their projects in marketing and sponsor relations. *The Big Issue in the North* (England) has developed an ongoing training partnership with Manchester United. The Spanish street paper *Milhistorias* has a partnership with Real Madrid. *Big News* from New York have developed links with the New York MetroStars. The Dutch team is connected with FC Utrecht. The organising street paper

Faktum in Gothenburg, reports higher sales and increased advertising revenue after the event.

The level of overall sponsorship for individual teams has doubled between the 2003 and 2004 events. There is a growing awareness about the positive aspects of sponsoring teams and the Homeless World Cup itself. Individual teams have also adopted a much more professional approach towards sponsorship, increasing support as a result.

All participating street papers and social organizations involved in the Homeless World Cup have formed football programmes on a regular basis as part of their overall social inclusion activities. The growing number of national qualifications and selections for the Homeless World Cup 2005 is a clear sign that the message from the tournament is being embraced at the grassroots levels amongst the participating nations. Twelve countries run or plan to develop a national street league for social inclusion projects after the Homeless World Cup in 2004. They include Austria, Denmark, France, England, Ireland, Poland, Scotland, Spain, Ukraine, Uruguay, USA and Wales. This represents an increase of 240% compared with 2003 when 5 countries organised street soccer leagues and a 400% increase since before the Homeless World Cup started in Graz in 2003.

As in other countries, there has been significant progress in Ireland. Mick Pender is very enthusiastic about the future.

"All but one of the players has moved on after Gothenburg. One even moved over to Gothenburg to be with someone he met during the World Cup. Another went into drug rehabilitation and is now doing two days a week at university while another is actually working with us as a social coach helping us to establish street soccer right across Ireland.

"We'll have a league across the whole country and the North of Ireland as well. Other projects are starting to wake up to the potential solution street soccer can bring and they are creating football teams. I know that you have a two year rule, where players cannot play for more than two years running, but we've cut that to one year in Ireland. You get one shot, that's it, and then you should be moving on."

In the course of our study, we had players add their comments. Here are just a couple, unedited:

"The good thing about the Homeless World Cup is that all the vendors can have the chance if they work at it. Anyway, they can meet people from other countries and you can notice how important it is for people. They really want to be stars of their lives. I think I am really a star now."

Sergio Peña, 26, Argentina.

"This is unforgettable. I realised I'm not alone. All those people there, with the same problem I have. They are rather confident and proud of themselves. Nevertheless, they don't have a permanent place to live – they feel positive. I came back here, to Ukraine, with a strong confidence to change my life. I understood that I'm the one, and the only one, who can change it. I looked at the girl who came with us, a young girl from the Way Home Fund, the journalist and translator, and understood one thing: if there are people who care about the homeless ones, I myself must be responsible for my life. I must be the first to take care of me. If it's important for those people what is happening with me (they are interested in me after the championship as well), this is me and only me who can do something and move forward."

Mykola Serebryansky, 31, Ukraine.

We are now moving forward with confidence. Sport has a huge potential to make a difference in the world. We've proved it and now have an obligation to take this to the next stage. But that's for the next book. In the meantime, get involved and change the world.

Viva football. Kick off homelessness.

APPENDIX ONE:

Graz 2003

The Squads

Austria

Ibu Ekwe	Desmond Ahanon
Samuel Osuji	Yaru Yaru Ibrahim
Jamba Sanesang	Angus Okanume
Nnadi Chibuike	Etienne Motaze

Coaches:
Dominic Emeka, Sigi Milchberger

Brazil

Adriano Alexandre da Silva	Caio Coimbra de Menezes
Daniel da Silva Souza Cunha	Wellington da Cunha Rodrigues
Judison Luiz Nascimento dos Reis	Leandro Santos da Silva
Max Junio Untaller	Nilo Marciano Coelho Júnior

Coaches:
Osmar Vargas de Oliveira/
Antonio Carlos Fernandes de Souza

Denmark

Stefan Karlsen	Orla Jensen
Tom Nielsen	Per Olsson
Michael Mathisen	Nehad Elia
Michael Jensen	Ole Claesson

Coach:
Lennart Boel/Jens Hojberg

England

Eric Houghton	Ian Cook
Craig Hodgson	Leon Francis
Darren Fazackerley	Mo Stevenson
Ismael Omar	Greg Joseph

Coaches:
Dave Bell, Louis Garvey

Germany

Florian Walther	Peter Skrabaut
Frank Papperitz	Carsten Kalischko
Christian Schneider	Klaus Bieda
Günther Bieda	Uwe Bröchiler

Coach:
Reinhard Kellner

Ireland

Patrick Murphy	Mark Hughes
Peter Farell	Peter White
Mark Bisset	Stephen Morgan
Mick Byrne	Michel Murphy

Coach:
Mike Pender/Jon Glackin

Italy

Emmerson Luiz Mendes dos Santos	Fereira Britto Fabiano
Daniel Valeriu Gibaru	Nicolae Barb
Garay Eduardo Marcelo	Souza Dos Santos Lucas Todeu
Rodrigo Rodrigues	Slataru Gheorghe Irinel

Coaches:
Gorgon Nojciech/Gordon Barbara/Kwappik Bogdan Jòzef

Netherlands

Elon van Tielenburg
Denis Schalwijk
Jan Boom
Teus Petersen
Tony van Dongen

Jeroen Sassen
Jeandro Baylin
Marcel Aertgerts
Huin Lloyd

Coaches:
Pim Doesburg/Sander de Kramer

Poland

Klaudiusz Jark
Rafael Betowski
Gregorz Kowalski
Kryzstof Czaplinski
Marisu "Orla" Orlowskiego

Marek Pawlak
Leszek Propokik
Michal Czaplinski
Jaroslaw Jaworski

Coach:
Jacek Czaplinski

Russia

Maxim Mastitski
Dzianis Chernoritsky
Andrej Li
Vitalij Shiskin

Yuri Kuzmin
Sergej Levchuk
Temir Trusynbekov

Coach:
Arkady Tiurin

Scotland

Thomas Comrie
Paul Baillie
Archie Murray
John McAnnany

Mark Elliot
Jason Elliot
Stewart Griffin
Michael Till

Coach:
Ian Sorby/Steve Hoy

Slovakia

Faro Olle jr
Stefan Malackj
Eva Rajcka

Jozef Jamrich
Fare Ole sen.

Coach:
Martin Opeta

South Africa

Mzwakhe Qutu
Bongani Mhlawuli
Meluxolo Taliwe

Nkosinathi Mkhonono
Themba Tinzi
Luyanda Konana

Coach:
James Garner

Spain

Modesto Bayon
Ángel Prados
Mariano Álvarez Aguado

José Vera Carlos
Jesús Urbano Juárez
Adolfo Conde

Coaches:
Miguel Buzeta, Ignacio Paniagua, Saúl Rodríguez

Sweden

Conny Lindenstrand
Leif Matsson
Björn Andersson
Hakan Olsson

Joakim Olsson
Hans Flory
Michael Sandberg

Coach:
Kenneth Sjökvist/Lena Pettersson

Switzerland

Mokhtar Ajman
Martin Strub
Urs Sauer
Miriam Evci-Thoma

Peter Gamma
Astrid Hagmann
Roger Meister
Peter Hässig

Coach:
Micheal Stegmaier

USA

Osvaldo Lebron
James Burch
Triton McEwan
Germain Santiago
José Riofrillo

Erick Rivera
Harris Pankin
Rory Levine
Jeff Rubins

Coach: Stephanie Quinn

Wales

Lee Richards
Brain Thomas
Glen Smith

Spencer Williams
John Fowler
Lee Jones

Coach: Keri Harris

Results 2003

Qualifying Round

Group A
Germany 0 : Netherlands 14
Sth Africa 10 : Wales 1
Germany 1 : Sth Africa 8
Netherlands 9 : Wales 0
Germany 1 : Netherlands 12
Sth Africa 3 : Wales 0
Netherlands 3 : Sth Africa 0
Germany 0 : Wales 1
Sth Africa 7 : Germany 1
Wales 3 : Netherlands 10
Wales 2 : Germany 1
Sth Africa 3 : Netherlands 8

Group B
Spain 2 : Sweden 7
USA 9 : Slovakia 4
Spain 11 : Switzerland 0
Sweden 6 : USA 5
Slovakia 9 : Switzerland 0
Spain 1 : USA 6
Sweden 8 : Slovakia 3
USA 10 : Switzerland 1
Spain 2 : Slovakia 3
Sweden 9 : Switzerland 0
Slovakia 5 : USA 6
Sweden 3 : Spain 2
Switzerland 2 : Spain 8
USA 1 : Sweden 4
Switzerland 1 : Slovakia 9
USA 2 : Spain 1
Slovakia 3 : Sweden 6
Switzerland 1 : USA 9
Slovakia : Spain cancelled.

APPENDIX ONE: GRAZ 2003

Group C

Russia 10 : Ireland 2
Denmark 1 : England 4
Russia 5 : Denmark 4
Ireland 1 : England 10
Russia 1 : England 7
Ireland 3 : Denmark 10
Ireland 1 : Russia 4
England 4 : Denmark 2
Denmark 7 : Russia 4
England 11 : Ireland 1
England 5 : Russia 3
Denmark 3 : Ireland 2

Group D

Poland 1 : Austria 5
Italy 6 : Brazil 9
Poland 5 : Scotland 7
Austria 4 : Italy 3
Brazil 4 : Scotland 3
Poland 2 : Italy 6
Austria 4 : Brazil 3
Italy 5 : Scotland 3
Poland 3 : Brazil 1
Austria 1 : Scotland 2
Brazil 6 : Italy 4
Austria 5 : Poland 3
Scotland 5 : Poland 3
Italy 5 : Austria 3
Scotland 1 : Brazil 7
Italy 4 : Poland 5
Brazil 3 : Austria 1
Scotland 1 : Italy 5
Brazil 3 : Poland 0
Scotland 0 : Austria 7

Intermediate Round

Group A, Group 1

Netherlands 8 : Sweden 1
Denmark 1 : Austria 9
Netherlands 21 : Slovakia 0
Sweden 5 : Denmark 8
Austria 26 : Slovakia 0
Netherlands 7 : Denmark 4
Sweden 0 : Austria 5
Denmark 10 : Slovakia 1
Netherlands 4 : Austria 2
Sweden 8 : Slovakia 0

Group A, Group 2

England 0 : Brazil 6
Sth Africa 5 : USA 2
England 6 : Italy 5
Brazil 4 : Sth Africa 5
USA 2 : Italy 12
England 5 : Sth Africa 0
Brazil 15 : USA 0
Sth Africa 1 : Italy 13
England 11 : USA 10
Brazil 3 : Italy 2

Group B, Group 3
Wales 4 : Spain 5
Ireland 4 : Poland 6
Wales 0 : Ireland 2
Spain 0 : Poland 15
Wales 1 : Poland 9
Spain 3 : Ireland 9

Group B, Group 4
Germany 4 : Switzerland 2
Russia 2 : Scotland 7
Germany 2 : Russia 11
Switzerland 0 : Scotland 13
Germany 1 : Scotland 10
Switzerland 4 : Russia 5

Finals Day Results
Scotland 3 : Poland 2
Russia 2 : Ireland 1
Germany 5 : Spain 8
Switzerland 4 : Wales 11
England 1 : Austria 2
Netherlands 4 : Brazil 1
Netherlands 1 : England 2
Austria 3 : Brazil 2
Italy 5 : Denmark 1
Sth Africa 4 : Sweden 2
USA 9 : Slovakia 5

Final Ranking: 2003 Graz
1 Austria
2 England
3 Netherlands
4 Brazil
5 Italy
6 Denmark
7 South Africa
8 Sweden
9 USA
10 Slovakia
11 Scotland (INSP Networking Trophy Winners)
12 Poland
13 Russia
14 Ireland
15 Spain
16 Germany
17 Wales
18 Switzerland (Fair Play Trophy Winners)

APPENDIX TWO:

Gothenberg 2004

The Squads

Argentina

Sergio Peña
Ruben Nunez
Alesandro Martinez
Matias Alvarez

Omar Paz
Lautaro Martinelli
Hector Hugo Gomez
Viktor Piris

Coach:
Sergio Rotman

Austria

Ali Gholami
Moshen Soltani
Poya Rezai
Manol Ivantschev

Ghasem Soltani
Akbar Rezai
Hassan Lashani
Safi Ahmad-Zubair

Coaches:
Martin Madlmayr/Gilbert Prilassnig

Brazil

Antonio Cesar Andrade da Silva
Claudio Bongiovani Azevedo
Irany Francisco dos Reis
Sergio Borges de Carvalho

Celso Pereira Possidonio
Dario Bertulucci
Marcos Jose Dias
Eduardo Fausto da Silva

Coaches:
Guilherme Vasconcelos de Araujo/Flavio Fernandes Rodrigues

Canada

William Leaman
David Arthey
Adrian Plowiec
Wesley Humphries

David Martin
Roger Freire
Darryl Lynk
Matthew Brown

Coach:
Paul Gregory

Czech Republic

Jiri Vancl
Stefan Malack
Jan Klime
Jan Okrucky

Martin Betu
Igor Kozen
Petr Blaha

Coaches:
Jiri Vancl/Petr Skaribiku

Denmark

Ibrahim Hamrauni
Verner Jeppesen
Per Olsson
Claudia Hoffensetz

Torben Gliese
Abdellatif Ahrouda
Kim Møller
Abbas Raza

Coach:
Lennart Boel

England

Ahmet Akdag
Kevin Wilson
Derrell Miller
Joe Torode

Adeleke Adenisi
Tony Sheerin
Auril Afrani
Alex Edwards

Coaches:
John Parrot, Eric Houghton

France

Stephan Paillart
Khelifi Belgarem
Alain Lossohmeau
Lamine Hamitouche

Rachid Obayt
Odeslati Tahar
Ahab Mouloud

Coach:
Dominique Poteau

Germany

Ekkehard Peters
Frank Papperitz
Markus Wetzel
Günther Bieda

Peter Skrabut
Detlef Wucherpfennig
Volker Schmitz
Uwe Bröckel

Coaches:
Dieter Hollnagel/Reinhard Kellner

Ireland

Patrick Murphy
Dermot Haverty
Keith McCarthy
Craig Douglas

Garett Henvey
Gerard Clifford
Anthony Nee
Peter Murphy

Coach:
Mike Pender

Italy

Alonso Hugo Marcello
Souza dos Santos Lucas Tadeu
Ocana Cortijo Paul Renato
Filippo Podesta

Garay Eduardo Marcelo
Rodrigo Stephenson Rodrigues
Armua Hector Ricardo
Gorgon Wojciech

Coaches:
Gorgon Barbara/Kwappik Bogdan Jòzef

Japan

Takahsi Ito
Kenichi Shimizu
Yasuharu Kwawharada
Nobuyuki Toritani

Tsugio Okawa
Yoshifumi Ito
Mitsuo Toyomura
Yoshinori Matsumoto

Coaches:
Satoru Ijiri, Tsuyoshi Katori, Yasunori Tsutsumi,
Rurika Naito Curtis

Netherlands

Demis Bol Sam
Hafid el Mattaoui
René de Laat
Fahad Abokor

John van Egdom
Hassan Boulouban
Hamid Boudih
Bob Wennekes

Coaches:
Thomas Jacometti/Stef Verplancke/
Reinder Schonewille/Gilly Brouwer

Namibia

Alfred Hendrik van Wyk
Josef Awaseb
Carlos Martin Nowaseb

Lesley Bam
Gioven Somseb
Lofty Lottering

Coaches:
Michaela Mittmann, Uirab Bethuel

Poland

Marek Sobczak
Sebastian Fabis
Andrej Krol
Sylwester Zwolinski

Roman Boguslawski
Lukasz Zdych
Pjotr Zaloga
Franciszek Woloszyk

Coach:
Artur Hyzyk/Jazek Czaplinski

Portugal

Paulo Silva
Candido Viera jr.
Carlos Fontes
Nelson Antunes

Jorge Rodriguez
Miguel Ribeiro
João Baião

Coaches:
João Boanabé, Vanda Ramalho, Paulo Marques,
Eduardo Reis

Russia

Evgeny Grigoriev
Ivan Malmygin
Arkady Tiurin
Dzianis Chernoritsky

Aleksandr Menus
Maxim Mastitski
Yuri Kuzmin
George Ngoume-Ngangue

Coach:
Arkady Tiurin

Scotland

Owen Turner
Kevin Stuart
Shawn Harris
Mark Elliot

Thomas Comrie
Philip Garden
David Duke
Robert Carney

Coach:
Ally Dawson

Slovakia

Michal Ondruek
Peter Kovač
Joshua Flynn
Oundrej Rysk

Peter Zaťko
Jurad Stojka
Jozef Jamrich

Coach:
Martin Opeta

South Africa

Mzwakhe Qutu
Mawande Jakalase
Ntobeko Makaula
Mfundo Ncapayi

Nkosinathi Mkhonono
Luzuko Bayi
Mziwamabhele Hlati
Bulelani Bambilahle

Coaches:
James Garner/Luvuyo Zahela

Spain

Rubén Martinez
Felix Bas
José Pablo Gallego
Juan Junco

Modesto Bayon
Isaac Negro
Juan Carlos Muñoz
Antonio Gómez

Coaches:
Miguel Buzeta, Ignacio Paniagua, Saúl Rodríguez

Sweden

Conny Lindenstrand
Tajmaz David Nilsson
Leif Matsson
Marvin Bajoumi

Joakim Olsson
Stefan Eliasson
Karl Erik Lith
Hans Flory

Coach:
Kenneth Sjökvist

Switzerland

Mokhtar Ajman
Peter Gamma
Raymond Grimaitre
Mario Hüssy

Rico Brunschwiler
Roland Füreder
Katrin Muntwyler
Rael Fiechter

Coaches:
Simone Burgherr/René Fiechter

Ukraine

Yevgen Ivanov   Yevgen Adamenko
Oleg Filatov   Mykola Serebryansky
Igor Malikin   Igor Zenov

Coach:
Valeriy Zavalniy

USA

Juan Contreras   Erick Rivera
Adrian Contreras   Jorge Lopez
Roberto Rivera   Abdul Rahim
Gerson Counou

Coach:
Braden Ferrari

Wales

Martin Ingram   Christopher Sartin
Sean Lewis   Lee Jones
Donovan Lawrence   Lee Anderson
Jason Cake   Sian Richardson

Coach:
Keri Harris/Kevin Davis/David Ormonde

Results 2004

1st Round

Group A
Austria 11: Canada 1
Canada 13 : Japan 1
Austria 10 : Japan 4

Group B
England 3 : Portugal 2
Portugal 3 : USA 6
England 4 : USA 3

Group C
Holland 1 : Poland 9
Poland 9 : Ireland 7
Holland 7 : Ireland 4

Group D
Brazil 8 : Slovakia 5
Cezch 2 : Scotland 6
Brazil 3 : Cezch 4
Slovakia 0 : Scotland 8
Slovakia 6 : Czech 3

Group E
Italy 17: Switzerland 0
Namibia 3 : Argentina 8
Italy 11 : Argentina 1
Switzerland 3 : Argentina 11
Italy 19 : Namibia 11
Switzerland 7 : Namibia 11

Group F
Denmark 5 : Spain 6
Spain 4 : Ukrain 6
Denmark 4 : Ukraine 2

Group G
Russia 14 : France 1
Sth Africa 3 : Russia 4
Sth Africa 3 : France 2

Group H
Sweden 7 : Germany 3
Germany 1 : Wales 4
Sweden 5 : Wales 1

Intermediate Upper

Group 1
Austria 5 : Italy 0
Wales 8 : Brazil 0
Austria 6 : Wales 0
Italy 12 : Brazil 0
Austria 9 : Brazil 3
Italy 5 : Wales 1

Group 2
England 2 : Denmark 1
Sth Africa 4 : Holland 1
England 3 : Sth Africa 6
Denmark 0 : Holland 16
England 6 : Holland 5
Denmark 1 : Sth Africa 0

Group 3
Poland 2 : Russia 4
Ukraine 3 : USA 6
Poland 8 : Ukraine 2
Russia 3 : USA 2
Poland 6 : USA 4
Russia 2 : Ukraine 5

Group 4
Scotland 5 : Sweden 3
Argentina 13 : Canada 5
Scotland 4 : Argentina 3
Sweden 7 : Canada 0
Scotland 12 : Canada 1
Sweden 5 : Argentina 3

INSP Network Cup

Golden Goal

Japan 5 : Ireland 15
Namibia 6 : France 5
Japan 3 : Czech 12
Ireland 9 : France 4
Namibia 8 : Czech 1
Japan 2 : Namibia 10
France 2 : Czech 1
Ireland 11 : Namiba 3
Japan 6 : France 10
Ireland 7 : Czech 2
Japan 3 : Ireland 11
Namibia 3 : France 1
Japan 3 : Czech 10
Ireland 4 : France 2
Namibia 6 : Czech 3
Japan 2 : Namibia 15
France 9 : Czech 0
Ireland 8 : Namibia 2
Japan 2 : France 12
Ireland 14 : Czech 0

Street Spirit

Portugal 10 : Slovakia 2
Spain 6 : Germany 2
Portugal 7 : Scotland 6
Slovakia 5 : Germany 10
Spain 9 : Switzerland 1
Portugal 8 : Spain 6
Germany 5 : Switzerland 2
Slovakia 2 : Spain 4
Portugal 11 : Germany 2
Slovakia 9 : Switzerland 8
Portugal 9 : Slovakia 2
Spain 1 : Germany 2
Portugal 7 : Switzerland 5
Slovakia 3 : Germany 1
Spain 8 : Switzerland 5
Portugal 5 : Spain 6
Germany 3 : Switzerland 6
Slovakia 3 : Spain 6
Portugal 11 : Germany 4
Slovakia 6 : Switzerland 7

Final Day

Semi Final

Ireland 4 : Spain 3
Namibia 1 : Portugal 2

Positions

Japan 4 : Slovakia 3
Czech 11 : Switzerland 3
France 5 : Germany 3
Spain 5 : Namibia 7

Final

Ireland 9 : Portugal 2

Factum Trophy
Hatrick
Wales 1 : Denmark 3
USA 15 : Canada 2
Wales 13 : Canada 1
Denmark 6 : USA 2
Wales 3 : USA 5
Denmark 17 : Canada 0
Wales 1 : Denmark 4
USA 12 : Canada 2
Wales 14 : Canada 1
Denmark 9 : USA 3
Wales 4 : USA 3
Denmark 14 : Canada 1

Team Spirit
Brazil 2 : Holland 8
Ukraine 9 : Argentina 5
Brazil 2 : Argentina 8
Holland 4 : Ukraine 5
Brazil 1 : Ukraine 8
Holland 9 : Argentina 8
Brazil 1 : Holland 14
Ukraine 6 : Argentina 4
Brazil 2 : Argentina 8
Holland 2 : Ukraine 6
Brazil 5 : Ukraine 14
Holland 6 : Argentina 4

Final Day
Semi Final
Denmark 2 : Holland 1
Wales 2 : Ukraine 3

Positions
Canada 0 : Brazil 5
USA 9 : Argentina 0
Holland 4 : Wales 6

Final
Denmark 3 : Ukraine 2

The Homeless World Cup

Group UN

Austria 1 : England 2
Poland 6 : Sweden 1
Austria 8 : Sweden 1
England 3 : Poland 5
Argentina 5 : Poland 2
England 8 : Sweden 1
Austria 3 : England 0
Poland 13 : Sweden 1
Austria 6 : Sweden 3
England 5 : Poland 3
Austria 5 : Poland 6
England 12 : Sweden 4

Group UEFA

Italy 6 : Sth Africa 2
Russia 5 : Scotland 2
Italy 9 : Scotland 4
Sth Africa 10 : Russia 3
Italy 2 : Russia 1
Sth Africa 4 : Scotland 5
Italy 3 : Sth Africa 0
Russia 2 : Scotland 3
Italy 11 : Scotland 3
Sth Africa 3 : Russia 2
Italy 3 : Scotland 0
Sth Africa 3 : Scotland 4

Semi Final

Austria 5 : Scotland 1
Poland 0 : Italy 5

Positions

Sweden 6 : Sth Africa 4
England 4 : Russia 5
Scotland 4 : Poland 7

Final

Austria 0 : Italy 4

Final Ranking : 2004 Gothenburg

1 Italy (Homless World Cup Champions)
2 Austria
3 Poland
4 Scotland
5 Russia
6 England
7 Sweden
8 South Africa
9 Denmark (Faktum Trophy Winners)
10 Ukraine
11 Wales
12 Holland
13 USA
14 Argentina
15 Brazil
16 Canada
17 Ireland (INSP Networking Trophy Winners)
18 Portugal
19 Namibia
20 Spain
21 France
22 Germany
23 Czech Republic
24 Switzerland
25 Japan (Fair Play Trophy Winners)
26 Slovakia